Dirty
Hands

JON STEFFES

i

ISBN:0615573576
ISBN-13:9780615573571

LCCN:

DEDICATION

For my wonderful wife, JoAnn, and my children,
Calvin, Kathryn, and Meghan.

ACKNOWLEDGMENTS

Thank you, JoAnn, for allowing me the opportunity
to write. None of this happens without your
love and support.

CHAPTER 1

CHARLIE TROUBLE

"Shhh!" Brian anxiously gestured toward me as he tried to pop the window open with his jackknife.

"Are you sure they're in there?" I asked nervously.

"Of course," Brian whispered back, his tongue sticking out as he concentrated on prying open the window.

"When have I ever steered you wrong," sneered Brian, "Now shut up before we get busted. Besides, I saw them get unloaded this afternoon." Brian confidently informed me in his wise-guy voice.

Not that Brian Wicka wasn't wise. Actually, he was probably pretty smart. He just didn't care. About school, about rules, and especially about what other people thought of him. He wasn't afraid to get in a fight either, most of the time for stupid reasons. Like three weeks ago, when Brian overheard Brad Spencer calling him a loser and that he cheated on his math test. Brian did pretty good in that fight. He *was* doing pretty good, had Brad on the ground defending himself from Brian's flurry of punches, when a couple of Brad's buddies jumped in. Brian's my best friend, probably my only friend, so I felt compelled to jump in too.

I'm smaller than any of them, normal height, but only about 100 pounds, so if Mr. Herbert, our 7th grade science teacher, hadn't broken it up, I probably wouldn't have lasted long, being as outnumbered as I was. I'm a pretty good fighter for my size, won a few, lost a few, but Brad and his buddies are all big football players, so a skinny loser like me can only do so much damage until getting over powered. Actually, Brian's not much bigger than I am. He's a bit shorter, but a lot stronger, with that "I hate your guts" attitude. When Mr. Herbert pulled everyone apart, Brian had a smile on his face. He got his shots in and was pretty happy about it. A little beat up, but pleased with his effort.

"Got it," Brian whispered as he popped open the window. "Hang onto this," he said calmly as he passed his knife back to me.

I stood up on the garbage can I was kneeling on, grabbed his knife, folded back the blade and put it in my pocket.

Brian grabbed the window sill, flexed his knees and using his arms to pull himself up, was able to get the upper half of his body into the window.

"Give me a push," Brian grunted.

I reached up and pushed until he wiggled his legs through the window frame. I heard a thump as he hit the floor on the other side. The thump was followed by a scraping sound as he pulled himself back up to the window frame. Then I heard his voice through the darkness.

"I'll grab something to stand on, on this side, and pass the boxes down to you," Brian whispered with confidence.

Then Brian disappeared from the window. I waited. The alley behind the appliance store was quiet, except for a couple of cars passing by on the street at the end of the alley. There were a couple of lights on in the old brick building across the alley from where I crouched on the metal garbage can.

"Where is *Brian*?" I wondered, becoming anxious. The voice in my head screamed, "Hurry up jerk!"

Out of the corner of my eye I saw a person pass by a lighted window in the building directly across from me. The person stood in the window for a moment, then moved out of sight.

"Did they see me?" I wondered, becoming panicky.

This wasn't the first time Brian's talked me into doing something stupid. Brian is known for his get rich quick schemes. I've known Brian since the first grade, and he started out by stealing Mrs. Anderson's polished rocks that outline her garden, painting weird faces on them, and selling them to his other neighbors as pet rocks. Innocent enough, I guess, except the rocks were stolen. We never got caught for that one. I think Mrs. Anderson knew it was us, but thought it was cute, some little six year old entrepreneurs. She even bought a rock from us.

But as Brian got older his schemes became larger, kept us out later at night, and usually involved some sort of trespassing. When we were in the sixth grade, we actually made some good money. We would hop the fence to the cemetery and hunt for night crawlers after a warm summer rain. We'd use our flashlights to spot the 'nighties' laying on the wet ground, half in, and half out of their holes.

Then Brian would grab them, pull them the rest of the way out slowly so as to not tear them in half, and put them in our bucket. My job was to carry the bucket. Riverside Bait paid us 25 cents a dozen for the night crawlers.

"Hey! What are you doing up there!?" I was brought back to attention by a light shining in my face, and the shadow of a man standing on the ground below me with a flashlight. While I was busy daydreaming, I had failed to see this guy walk through the alley and right up to me.

"I said, what are you doing up there? Get down now!" This time his voice held authority.

I looked at him, not able to see him clearly, with the light shining in my eyes. I didn't know what to do. Glancing across the alley, I could see the lighted window where I saw the person before. The silhouette of a person was again in the window, obviously watching the scene below. The man with the light moved the beam of the flashlight up to where the open window was directly above me. As he did this, the light was, for a moment, out of my eyes, and I could see the man's uniform. A cop. I suddenly felt sick to my stomach. The cop started talking on his radio. He was only ten feet away, and I could hear everything he said.

"I have a kid perched on a garbage can below an open window in the alley between 4th and 5th Streets, a block east of Franklin."

The crackly sound of reply came from his radio. I remained in my crouch unsure what to do. Do I jump down and run? Do I say something? My face felt warm and sweat began to bead on my forehead.

"Directly behind the Appliance Mart warehouse….in the alley," came more directions from the officer to his radio.

Speaking directly at me in a hushed voice, light still in my face, he said, "O.K. kid, who's in the building?" The officer motioned for me to come down and reached to his hip.

To borrow one of Brian's sayings, "when in doubt, run!"

When the cop motioned for me to come down, instead of clambering down and surrendering, I leapt to my left off the garbage can. Landing on both feet, I stumbled briefly in my attempt to hit the ground running, using my hands to push myself off the alley gravel, and took off running.

"Hey!" I could feel the breeze of the cop's arms swipe just behind me as he yelled out and tried to grab me.

As I ran I could hear behind me the cop reporting the direction I was heading on his radio. I sprinted down the dark alley lined with old brick building, big green garbage dumpsters, and loading docks. As I ran, I could hear the cop, running about 20 short feet behind me, yelling for me to stop, and cursing me out. I made short work of the alley, running to the end in a matter of seconds. I was just about to the street, when a squad car pulled into the alley ahead of me. I had just enough time to swerve, avoided getting hit by the car, and rushed between the driver's side door and a building just before the cop in the car opened his door to stop me. I hung a quick right turn and flew down the sidewalk, crossed the street, then turned left down another street. As I ran around the corner, I could hear the squad car's door close, reverse out of the alley, and its tires squeal as it took off after me.

By now I could no longer hear the first officer who was on foot behind me, and I wasn't about to turn around for a look. A block down, I was starting to slow from a sprint to a paced run. As I crossed the next street, a police car rounded the corner and came toward me. Looking toward the car, I could see that both officers were in the car now. If I could make it one more block to my right, I could make it to the woods that bordered the river behind a couple factories and warehouses. I dodged between two parked cars on the dark street, and ran between two buildings. I was now off the street and heading across a vacant lot, the tall weeds growing up grabbed at my legs trying to take me down. Behind me, I heard the door slam as one of the cops jumped out to continue the chase on foot. But I had a good lead on him, and was more worried about having to cross the next street over and make it to the industrial park that contained a couple old buildings, an occasional woodlot, and the river directly behind. I hoped that I could lose them in the woods. Sirens could be heard nearby. With my heavy breathing and feet slamming hard on the ground as I ran, they sounded like they were all around me. I needed to cross the next street before they cut me off. I knew that if I made it to the industrial park, they would have no choice but to follow me on foot. My lungs burned as I continued on, but I felt my odds were good of outrunning some old cop in a foot race.

As I neared the street I could see the cop car that was chasing me round the corner and head my way. I poured it on and crossed just ahead of it. I then heard the screech of tires as the police car slammed on the brakes and the driver get out. Suddenly I saw another cop car to my right driving across the vacant lot in my direction. A fence was between us separating the lot from the factory property I was running across. I couldn't stop now, even though my legs were starting to feel heavy and my breath was coming in gasps. If I could keep a big enough lead between me and the cops running behind me, to get over the fence and into the woods, I was home free. Only 30 yards from the fence, I saw that I was going to make it to the fence ahead of the officers behind me on foot and the car, which was having trouble going fast across the rough terrain of the vacant lot. I poured it on, my lungs burning, but feeling confident I could escape this mess Brian got me into. When I was a few feet from the fence, I jumped, and using my feet, toes dug into the chain link fence, grabbed the top metal bar. My legs felt heavy as I pulled myself up to straddle the top. For the first time in the race I looked back at the cops chasing me on foot. There were two now, and they were farther back than I thought, a good 50 yards, but still coming. I pulled my leg over the top of the fence catching my calf on the top, sharp point of the fence. I felt the sting as I pulled my leg over. The fence was probably eight feet high, yet I jumped to the ground, rolled as I hit the ground, scrambled to my feet and ran through the tall grass into the woods.

Unsure if anyone was following me, I kept going, yet now at a jog. Once I was a little way into the woods, I turned to again look behind me. I couldn't see anyone, but

I could see flashlight beams flashing about near the fence. Time to find somewhere to hide and to catch my breath I thought to myself. I made my way through the woods to the river. In case one of the cops was ambitious enough to jump the fence and look for me, I moved slowly and tried to be as quiet as possible. I didn't have to go far into the woods until I could see the river. As I got closer to the water, I started to recognize some landmarks. The cement channel marker that stood at the water's edge was to my left. I could also make out the buoy that marked the other side of the navigable channel a good 200 yards straight out from me. I made my way along the rocky shoreline.

Brian had taken me fishing along this shoreline many times, and sometimes while we were supposed to be in school, so I knew of an old boat that was chained to metal supports of the cement channel marker. I headed for the boat. I could hide under it. I crawled under it, smelling a combination of dead fish and stagnant water. The boat was a 14 foot aluminum, probably used by some fisherman, flipped upside down to keep out the rain, and laying amongst the rocks that lined the river bank to keep the river from washing away the bank during the high water in the springtime. Using a chain, a person would keep the boat attached to a tree, rock, or something else solid, so all that had to be done was to carry the outboard motor, gas tank, and gear down to the river's edge, flip the boat over, shove it into the water, and take off. Judging by the many dents and scratches, the boat had seen plenty of use.

The ground under the boat was muddy. I had to crawl to get under the boat but was quickly able to sit, hunched a bit, under the boat. Listening, I didn't hear anybody following me.

I looked at the mud on my hands and began to feel uneasy. There was something about getting dirty; I couldn't stand it. I always hated to have my hands dirty. I hated the sandy, gritty feeling, and having dirt under my finger nails. Brian thought I was such a baby. He always laughed at me when he took me fishing, and I was constantly washing my hands off in the river. I would only agree to go fishing with him if he baited my hook and took off the fish. He teased me, but that is one of the main reasons Brian is my best....and probably only friend, I felt comfortable enough around him to let him see my compulsions.

I wasn't under the boat for more than two minutes before the mud and sand on my clothes and in particular, my hands, forced me to crawl back out. My anxiety grew each second my hands remained dirty. Luckily, the boat was only feet from the river's edge. I quickly stooped to wash my hands. I tried to wash quietly, first my hands, then my arms, then my face. I made great effort to spend the same amount of time washing each limb....another of my compulsions.

While washing, I began hearing voices coming from the direction of where I jumped the fence, and, down the river's edge farther toward the direction I had been heading before stopping at the boat. Scanning the bank in the dark, I had to make a decision quickly as to what to do. The strip of woods along the river was narrow, only about 100 feet wide, and I needed to head in the direction of the voices, but that would be difficult, even in the dark. I considered swimming across the river for a moment. I was on the school's swim team, and even though I was only going into 8th grade, I knew I could make it. But decided not to chance it in the dark.

A tree. I needed to get into a tree. Most of the big trees along the shoreline were down, but in the woods away from the rocky shoreline. I found one right away. I leaped up, grabbed one of the thick lower branches, and pulled myself up. It was easy to climb higher. I got comfortable, and relaxed, still sweating from the run and the nervousness of my situation. I reached down in the dark to feel, through the tear in my jeans, my left calf that I scraped on the fence. It was hard to tell what was sweat, and what was blood. The stinging in my leg as my hand touched the cut confirmed my injury. It didn't feel too deep. The pain was probably mostly from the sweat invading the cut. I couldn't help also rubbing my right calf. Another of my habits. If I itch my left arm, I also have to itch my right arm, whether it actually itches or not. I can't help it. I just have to do it.

I sat for nearly an hour by the river in the tree. The cops stumbled around in the dark shining their flashlights everywhere in the woods around me, but never where I perched, fifteen feet up in a tree. I finally climbed down. I was anxious to hear what happened to Brian, and to get some light to see how big of a cut I had on my leg. I didn't bleed too much. But with all the mud and sweat in the cut, it burned something awful.

Brian had told me that getting chased by cops was a "Rush," I disagree. As I walked home all I could think of was how scared I was during the chase, how lucky I was to get away, and how much Brian's schemes were starting to annoy me.

CHAPTER 2

BRIAN – HIS VERSION

"If each of us can carry two stereos in boxes, and we could sell them for $100 a piece in school, that's $400. Charlie worries too much. This will be easy and besides I'll split the money with him," Brian thought to himself.

"Now, if Charlie keeps look out and I could only get this window open, we're in the money," Brian continued plotting.

"Are you sure they're in there?" Charlie asked.

"Of course, when have I ever steered you wrong!" Brian whispered back to Charlie as he pried open the window with his knife.

Brian had seen trucks pull through the alley, bringing boxes to this warehouse many times, and it was easy to tell that all the boxes contained stereos and TVs and other electronics. He figured they probably store them in the warehouse until the stores are ready for them.

When Brian managed to squeeze through the window, he hit the ground on the other side, knocking the wind out of himself. He had to wait a minute or so, not just to catch his breath, but so his eyes could adjust to the dark. He wanted to use his flashlight as little as possible.

Brian always got a rush from doing stuff at night, whether it was sneaking onto a golf course at night to drag the ponds with a bicycle basket for golf balls, or visiting cemeteries on rainy nights to pull night crawlers. All these things Brian would do with Charlie, and always in an attempt to make some money. Of course, Charlie usually worried too much, and he didn't really need the money. Charlie's dad was rich, and, Brian knew he'd give Charlie anything he wanted just so he'd stay out of his hair and let him work.

"I don't have a rich dad," Brian thought to himself as he moved in the dark warehouse.

In fact, Brian hadn't seen his dad for five years, since he was nine years old. He wasn't even sure where he was. His mom wouldn't tell him when he asked.

"Don't worry about it. Trust me, it's not worth worrying about," His mom would say.

If his mom didn't care, then Brian wouldn't care either. But getting money to buy things wasn't as easy as it was for Charlie. If he needed a new pair of shoes, he'd have to find a way to get it. That's what brought him to the warehouse, in downtown Minneapolis at two o'clock in the morning.

"Be right back," Brian whispered down to his panicky friend, squatting below the window on a garbage can.

He began walking slowly toward a row of huge shelves, sort of like the ones in grocery stores, but much bigger. As his eyes continued to adjust to the darkness, he could see that the warehouse was big, lined with aisles of big shelves, all holding boxes of all sizes. He could see the glowing exit signs quite a distance away. Brian's eyes strained in the dark to read the words on a row of boxes.

Brian hoped Charlie was doing his job out in the alley. All he had to do was keep a look out so he could grab what he needed and get out. He was actually surprised Charlie was willing to come along. But, even when Charlie would balk at his ideas, he was always easy to convince. A couple taunts like "Don't be a chicken!" or, the one that always seemed to work, "Fine, stay home and wash your hands," is all that it took.

As Brian continued to search for the stereo boxes he wanted, he thought about his friend Charlie. Brian had never seen a guy who liked to wash his hands as much as Charlie. He'd taken him dragging for golf balls, fishing, and pulling night crawlers. All great money-makers. Every time Brian turned around the crazy guy was rinsing his hands off in the water. Night crawler pulling was really a challenge for Charlie. Brian did all the work. He was the one on his hands and knees in the dirt, grabbing the worms. Charlie would carry the bucket. That's all he had to do. But still he always had the container of baby wipes in his back pocket. If water wasn't available, he'd have the wipes. Brian tried not to rib him too much normally, just when he needed to convince him of something. Charlie, for a kid who got everything he needed, was really a miserable kid. It was just him, his dad, and his nanny. His dad worked a ton, and with Charlie being so weird, he didn't do so well making friends. Brian liked him though, especially on nights like tonight, when he needed someone to watch his back.

"Bingo!" Brian said softly when he spied the boxes he wanted. A box with a stereo inside. The small, stackable ones. Easy to carry, and, as he hoisted one from the shelf, light enough to carry two at a time. Carefully, he lowered the first box to the floor. Once Brian had the second box stacked on top, he stooped to lift them both. He made his way to the window moving slowly, feeling his way in the dark with each step.

"Charlie," Brian sharply whispered when he arrived under the window he had squeezed through only minutes before.

"Charlie…..Charlie," he whispered again louder.

"Where is he?" Brian wondered. "Either he can't hear me or he chickened out and took off."

Setting the boxes down, Brian searched for something to place under the window to stand on. The bottom of the window frame was about six feet off the floor, probably more for light during the day than for looking out of. Finding a pallet and leaning it against the wall, Brian was clambering up to the window, bracing his feet on the wooden pallet, hands on the window ledge about to pull himself up when he heard the shouts.

"Hey, what are you doing up there!" came the shouts from outside the window in the alley. More voices and shouting and Brian came down from the pallet, moving away from the window inside the warehouse, trying to listen to the events unfolding outside.

"Was it the police? Were they after Charlie?" All these thoughts hit him as Brian stood in the warehouse, considering what to do.

17

When the voices and shouts stopped, Brian began to again climb the side of the pallet to the window. As his hands caught hold of the ledge and he braced his legs to push himself up, the beam of a flashlight hit him, a split second before the hands grabbed his legs.

The struggle against the officers was short. They even laughed a little at how Brian wouldn't give up easily as they escorted him out of the warehouse. They asked him some questions about why he was there and who his friend was that ran off. Brian knew then that Charlie had managed to get away. Brian provided them with no answers, refusing to talk. He even got to listen to some of the radio conversation of the officers giving chase while sitting in the back of the squad car.

Brian couldn't help grinning a little bit. He didn't know whether to be happy for Charlie or mad because Charlie had left his spot on the garbage can and got him busted.

CHAPTER 3

THE POLICE

I woke up to the sound of a group of people talking downstairs. I rolled over and looked at the clock....10:30 a.m. I figured it must be some of my dad's rich clients, another wealthy guy seeking the advice of Steven Jamison, investment counselor. His clients would often come over to my house so my father could tell them how to get even richer.

I had managed once again to sneak in the house through a window in the basement. That was always my way in and out of the house when I snuck out to hang with Brian. Sneaking in and out of the house may have been difficult if I lived in a smaller house, but I lived in a huge, three story house. The house was an old house, once lived in by some rich guy in the late 1800's. It was actually a pretty cool house. The whole property was surrounded by an iron fence and big shrubs grew up around the whole house, which only helped to conceal my comings and goings. My dad and I only talked when he had time, which wasn't very often. He was always busy buttering up his clients, often over dinner, so he sometimes didn't come home from work until well after dinner.

Being the only child with a dad who is a workaholic and living in a big house can be pretty lonely at times. Jane was our housekeeper and, even though I hate the term, my nanny. I hated the idea of having a nanny; it made me feel like such a baby, not like the usual thirteen year olds I went to school with. When Brian would come over to pick me up to go do something, he often said, "better make sure it's O.K. with your *Nanny*," really sarcastically. It drove me nuts. Brian never came into the house. He knew how much my dad disliked him, and besides, I think in Brian's eyes, the world was full of things to try to get away with, and people to challenge.

Suddenly, my bedroom door opened. Rolling over to tell my dad to let me sleep, I saw that it wasn't my dad. Two police officers swiftly came over to my bed and grabbed me by my arms.

"Charles Jamison, you have the right to remain...."

The next thing I knew, I was sitting in the back of a squad car. They told me that I was being charged with being an accomplice to felony breaking and entering. They told me I was going to go with them to the police station where I would be questioned and charged. They told me I was hanging around with the wrong people. They told me that by the looks of my house, I seemed to have everything I could need, what in the world was I doing breaking into warehouses. They told me that my dad was worried sick and concerned about me. They told me all those things that I didn't want to hear.

I believed them about everything except the last thing, about my dad. When the police officers were waiting for me to put some clothes on for the ride to the police station, my dad didn't even come into my bedroom to help me get out of that mess. He sat in the hallway and waited…probably hoping they'd hurry up so he could get to a meeting or something. And as I looked behind me, out the back window of the squad car, I didn't see him following behind. I guess, as usual, I was on my own, fending for myself.

The eight day wait until I had to go to court wasn't much fun. Being confined to the house in the summer was a combination of loneliness and frustration. Of course, my dad was busy at work, which suited me just fine. Jane was put in charge of keeping an eye on me and making sure I didn't leave the house. Lying around in my room, sulking, I had time to think. Dad had mainly just lectured to me on how disappointed he was; how since mom died life was tough enough without me doing stupid stuff with Brian.

I was pretty bent out of shape at Brian for rolling over on me and turning me in. Brian had called the night after his arrest to beg forgiveness.

"Come on Charlie!" Brian tried with his wise guy voice, "What was I supposed to do?"

"You didn't have to tell them that I was with you!" I had protested.

"I had no choice, man," Brian muttered.

His voice had been shaky, like he may have been on the verge of crying. It was something I had not heard before. Brian sounding rattled? Scared? I had paused, not knowing what else to say, not because I didn't feel like arguing, like telling Brian how I wish our friendship was

21

more than running around breaking rules, but because when Brian sounded scared....it made me scared. It made me realize that maybe it was actually more serious than I had thought.

I had my arms crossed behind my head, staring at the ceiling. Many thoughts concerning Brian flooded my mind. I knew he was my only real friend. I began to think that maybe Brian knew that I was his only friend as well. I knew other guys at school, of course. Being on the swim team, I had plenty of opportunities to interact with other kids. But, for some reason, I just always preferred to hang in the background.

I couldn't help having a mixture of feelings: scared about what the judge may decide; angry that I let Brian get me into this mess; and nervous that our friendship may be forced to an end, when I knew making new friends wasn't exactly my field of expertise. Maybe I should have been happy that I wouldn't be able to hang out with Brian anymore. That made me more scared than anything else.

Brian recognized and accepted my quirks, many of which my dad failed to notice. It all started with what made me feel comfortable and what made me nervous. For instance, if you looked at my bedroom, you would think that I was just a neat freak, had just moved in, or wasn't into clutter. But if you took the time to look at the little I have for décor, you'd see what I always hoped people would miss.

My room was a perfect square, which was relieving to me. I'm a bit obsessed with symmetry. Too many corners, and I wouldn't be able to sleep. My bed was centered with the headboard exactly equal distance from both side walls. Perched on the headboard, which also contained a bookshelf with sliding doors, I had one family picture, centered of course. On the wall that ran flush with the headboard, hung two pictures.....same size, same distance between the wall and headboard. My obsession to having things equal on both sides of everything extended to the pictures as well.

When our nanny/housekeeper, Jane, first started working for us, she just thought I was boring. She saw the bare white walls and decided to take me shopping. It was shortly after my mom died, so she was trying hard to help me out.

"We need to get you some nice posters or something for your room," She had told me.

Jane took me to a sporting goods store and tried to convince me to buy some sports posters, but I wasn't interested. I finally settled on two pictures of exactly the same size, square shaped, both pictures of sailing ships. And, as you may have guessed by now, the boat in the picture faced right while positioned to the left of my headboard, and the boat in the picture faced left while positioned to the right of the headboard. It didn't take long for Jane to begin noticing that I had more than a few quirky obsessions.

School had just gotten out for the summer. Usually, I would have been out having fun, or at least following Brian around, fishing, or at least watching Brian fish. We would also go to the YMCA on Main Street to play foosball and ping pong. Everything was free there. Brian never had any money, so unless I wanted to flip the bill, the "Y" was a good choice. I had access to plenty of money. Dad would give me as much as I wanted. It was always easier to give me money so I could get out the house and do things, especially in the summer. Otherwise, I would hang close to home and drive Jane nuts, and dad, if he was working from home. If it was a day dad was working from home, money was easy to get, a few bucks to stay out of his hair.

It was a long eight days but my day in court finally came.

CHAPTER 4

STEVE JAMISON

Things had been hard on Steve Jamison the last few years. First, Karen, his wife died five years ago. The battle with cancer had been a short one, but painful nonetheless. Steve fought with the deep sadness that comes from losing the one you love. Karen was fabulous; bright and caring, working as a nurse and showing Steve the same gentle nature that she shared with her patients. Charlie on the other hand, barely wept. Instead he withdrew. Charlie's reaction to his mother's sickness was at first fear, then when she lost the fight against cancer, his emotions changed to anger, and, Steve thought, hatred towards his father.

Next, Steve had to battle his own depression, only kept at bay by his focus on work, trying to succeed financially, trying to keep all his hard work going in the right direction.

Finally, Steve had to deal with Charlie. When the police officers showed up one morning to collect Charlie, it was like dealing with Karen's death all over again.

When the officers went into Charlie's room to wake him and lead him out, Steve couldn't go in. He waited in the hall, too struck by the event unfolding in front of him. Charlie went willingly; no protesting and no tears.

He knew Charlie had been causing trouble in the last year or so. Small things. A neighbor coming over to say Charlie had been throwing snowballs at cars, or a call from school telling him that Charlie had gotten into a scuffle with another boy. But never the police. Steven found himself unsure which direction to turn. His first instinct was to jump in his car and follow Charlie to the police station. But, maybe a little scare would help straighten Charlie out. What would his Karen have done if she were alive? She would have made sure her son was taken care of. She probably wouldn't have let Charlie get into this mess to begin with, but she would have thought rationally. Robert Phelps, Steven's lawyer, he would help. The squad car was already down the block and out of sight, when Steven hopped into his car, cell phone in hand. As he began driving, he tried Robert's number. He got his voicemail. Steven changed course as he drove to catch up with the squad car. Instead, he turned toward Robert's house.

His son's trouble's had seemed to grow and grow every year since his mother's death, and Steven felt that this may be the final blow.

CHAPTER 5

THE DRIVE

The stretch of interstate between Minneapolis and southern Minnesota was driven without any talk. My father stared straight ahead. I glanced at him a couple times and could see the muscles in his jaw flexing, his clenched teeth compressing, something he often did when he was upset, which lately, was quite often. Even the congested traffic and the crazy drivers sharing his road weren't enough to cause a reaction. His usual grumbling about traffic was aborted. My head rested on my hand, my elbow on the door's armrest, eyes out the window. I didn't feel like talking either.

I had been told very little about what we were going to be doing for the next week. My father had only told me that we were going to visit my Uncle Mark in Cedar Bluff, Minnesota. It had been a long time since I had seen Mark, years probably. He did some farming and construction work, I knew that much, but since my mom died, my father had lessened his contact with his brother.

It wasn't until we jumped on Interstate 90 that my father seemed to relax enough to talk.

"Charles, you have to believe me, this is for the best," my father said, only glancing at me briefly.

I continued to look out the window, feeling my face warm with nervousness and resentment, knowing he was going to keep going, and I wasn't sure I wanted to hear it. My father continued, "We caught a break with the police. You were lucky; the judge decided that you did not need to go to a juvenile facility, and agreed to Robert's requests that you get away from the city and that *friend* of yours..."

I huffed a little at the tone attached to the word 'friend'. At first I had been mad at Brian for creating this mess. But during the last couple of weeks, sitting around the house alone, I had started to miss him. Maybe it was out of boredom, maybe it the realization that there wasn't any other friend for me to do things with. I couldn't have had a friend come over the house if I wanted to. I just wasn't close to anybody else. I had started to realize that Brian was all I had.

My father didn't like my response when he mentioned Brian and that got him going even more.

"Every time you and Brian get together......you end up doing something you're not supposed to. Before you started hanging around him, you never got detention at school. You had other, normal friends. People weren't coming to our door saying you threw snowballs at their car, and you weren't going in front of a judge for breaking and entering."

"Brian went inside, not me," I mumbled.

"See!" my father snapped at me, "You even admit it. Brian is the source of most of your problems. You just said so yourself."

"It would probably help if I had a mother," I mumbled again with an indignant tone of my own.

"Charles," my father said pleadingly, "You can't blame this on your mother. You chose to dirty your hands with this behavior; you're mother, or her death, had nothing to do with it."

I couldn't think of a good response to that. I knew he was right. Brian had sort of lead the charge in our activities, most of which were different that most 13 year olds I knew, and that I hung around with before becoming so connected with Brian. I figured I better shut up for a while.

I must have fallen asleep. The slam of my father's car door woke me with a start. We had stopped at a gas station. I sat up straight to look around out the window.

Seeing me awake, my father opened his door, "I just need to fill up and then we'll find a place to stop and grab a bite to eat."

He paused, just about to shut his car door, "Charlie....you'll like Mark, and....this is temporary. We were able to avoid harsher consequences with the judge by doing this. I'll stay for a couple days with you at Mark's, but then I need to head back home to take care of some business."

My father had told the judge that I was going to stay with relatives back home, in his hometown. He had been able to convince the judge that a change of scenery would help me and that I would benefit from being in the country and away from other boys, namely Brian, that were leading me astray. I think we were both nervous about where this whole thing would take us.

I didn't answer him. Not looking at him, I managed to nod slightly in agreement. He was right about Mark. It had been over a year, but I remembered him. He was pretty cool. He wasn't like my dad. My dad is stuffy, a suit and tie guy. We had only seen Mark two times since my mom died. One time was at the funeral. Then a couple years after that we saw Mark when he spent a weekend with us. Both times, Mark looked uncomfortable in the dress clothes he was wearing, uncomfortable in our house, and even uncomfortable around my dad. He loosened up around me a bit. He told me about his farm and about the small streams that fed the Mississippi River running past his town, Cedar Bluff. Cedar Bluff was where my dad and Mark grew up. I was there less than a dozen times, mostly when I was young, again, before my mom died. We were going there now, I was to stay with Mark, temporarily, but I had a feeling things would be a lot different than when I was ten.

CHAPTER 6

MARK IN CEDAR BLUFF

The wipers worked rhythmically on Mark's old Chevy as it worked its way down Winnebago Creek Road on the way to town, water splashing up as the truck hit the many potholes in the gravel.

The phone call from Steve in Minneapolis last night was a rare event. Since Steve's wife died after a short battle with cancer, the phone calls all but stopped. Mark saw it as an indication of Steve's sadness and of his desire to work through it. Contact with Mark and home undoubtedly brought back memories of Karen. Karen was born and raised in the same town of Cedar Bluff, Minnesota, as Mark and Steve Jamison. The beauty of the small Mississippi river town, with its hardwood bluffs and valleys funneling creeks into the big river, created a wonderful place to grow up. Steve had been the charismatic athlete. He was a leader in all aspects of his youth. He had been the quarterback on the football team, pitcher on the baseball team, and steady scorer on the basketball court. His grades in school were good, if not great. Steve was involved in Student Council and other high profile activities to go along with his sports. Steve was a popular guy in a small town, a big fish in a little pond. He could have had his pick of girlfriends, but he only had eyes for Karen. She was beautiful, tall, and slim with long brown hair that seemed to shine. Her brown eyes revealed a trusting, kind-hearted soul. Steve and Karen were never far apart. They stayed that way, and were married, shortly after college.

Mark came to the end of the gravel road and turned left onto the county road. The drive into town usually only took 20 minutes, but the recent late spring rains had added to the potholes on Winnebago Creek Road's gravel surface so a few extra minutes were added to the trip. That was O.K. with Mark. He needed time to process what he needed for his brother's visit. Since Karen's death five years ago, Steve had immersed himself into his work, and removed himself from keeping up with his family. A phone call from Steve had become pretty rare, a visit even more so. With Steve working so much, even though he was financially successful, he wasn't having the same success keeping tabs on his son, Charlie. Charlie had been hanging around with the wrong type of kids. He had been in trouble from time to time, not anything major, throwing snowballs at cars, that sort of thing. But Mark had talked to Steve that morning on the phone and things sounded serious. Steve didn't know what to do. He asked Mark to look after him until he could sort some things out. Mark would oblige. He missed his brother and hoped his sorrow would go away soon.

Mark slowed his truck to a stop in front of Harris's Grocery. The old Chevy had been Mark's baby for more than fifteen years. The green paint had long since faded, and it showed the signs of years of hauling wood, supplies for Mark's new little farm, and a few bigger dents from sliding off the road into trees during the snowy Minnesota winters.

Mark, on the other hand was in excellent shape. Thirty-six years old, Mark was different than his older brother. He preferred to keep a low profile. A good athlete like Steve, however, Mark liked to focus his activities around hunting and fishing. Growing up in the Mississippi River valley brought him access to excellent hunting and fishing only minutes from town. Mark grew up spending his time working odd jobs, and spending his money on his outdoor interests. At over six foot tall and 220 pounds with dark curly hair, Mark was a solid figure as he climbed out of his truck to enter the grocery store. His faded blue jeans and equally faded yellow t-shirt, brought out the color in his tan, strong arms. He loved Cedar Bluff. It had everything he had wanted as a youth and was the place he chose to live as an adult.

However, everything became a bit more difficult when grown up. Steve had gone off to college, and their parents had done as much as possible to contribute financially to Steve's college education. They threw much of their savings at Steve, determined that he make it through college, something they never were able to do. By the time Mark graduated from high school, the well had run dry; they didn't have anything left to offer Mark. At first he was bitter. Why should Steve, the star quarterback, the charismatic one, get all the breaks, and the chance to go to college?

It didn't take Mark long to get past his bitterness. If his parents couldn't afford to help him get to college, he would take a year to work, save some money and go the following year. He enjoyed his freedom. No high school classes to bog him down and keep him inside. He took a job working for a farmer, Addison Torgelson, a kind old man who took Mark under his wing. He loved the work. He enjoyed being responsible for the cows, helping to milk them, feed them, and taking care of the many other duties in the milk parlor. His jobs around the farm, where he could be outdoors, were what he liked best. Being on his feet, able to move around, appealed to Mark. A desk job wasn't in his plans. He had thought about applying to the University of Minnesota and working on becoming a veterinarian, but the thought of several years of study couldn't bring him to take care of the paperwork. While he worked for Mr. Torgelson in the afternoons and evenings, he spent his mornings working for his uncle at the Coulee Lumber Company. Mark worked from 6:00 a.m. to 11:00 a.m. each day using a head saw to produce rough cut lumber from logs. Five hours a day waiting for his chance to get outside at Torgelson's farm. But that was more than a dozen years ago. After his parents died, a year apart of each other, Mark decided the life he was living wasn't enough for him. He wanted to be his own boss. The inheritance was small, but Mark, tired of working for someone else, combined that money with the money he saved to buy his own farm, a small farm, only 64 acres, most of it wooded, but it was a start. He knew he needed more acreage. He took a job working for a business in La

Crosse, just across the river in Wisconsin, installing laminate flooring hoping to make more money. He wanted the job to be temporary.

His goal was to grow apple trees in the upper end of his valley, and on some land he hoped to acquire from a neighbor, but saving money was a slow process. He would be patient. But, life was getting better. Now, instead of going home every night to his little upstairs apartment above a friend's garage, he went home to his farmhouse, surrounded by the bluffs, and with Winnebago Creek flowing by his house. He was happy.

Mark was not ready to have company for the weekend, let alone his nephew stay with him for the summer. The spare room in Mark's old farmhouse was storage, needing to be cleaned out for company, and he badly needed groceries. Mark had jotted down a list of items he needed at Harris's Grocery.

"Mark! Good to see you! How are things?!" cried Margie Harris, peering around a short man standing at the counter, as she rang up his items at the till.

Mark strode over to the counter and received a hearty handshake and slap on the back from Buster Roberts, a local fix-it-all man.

"You been hidin'? Haven't seen you in ages!" exclaimed Buster.

Buster was a mason by trade, but he had expanded to roofing, building sheds, framing in garages, and just about anything else anybody needed.

"Keepin' busy," said Mark with a warm smile for his friend. Giving Buster a quick look up and down and seeing his sawdust covered jeans and t-shirt, "Looks like you been busy!"

"Been rebuilding Dennis Taylor's garage roof, tree fell on it last week during that storm," Buster replied as he wiped off the sawdust.

"Well, I need to do some scrambling," Mark said with a sigh, as he addressed both Margie and Buster, "Steve's coming into town. Bringin' his son."

"Steve! That's wonderful!" exclaimed the always perky Margie Harris.

"Haven't seen much of Steve since…well…," said Buster, looking down, feeling bad about bringing up Steve's past tragedy.

"Yeah, he hasn't been up to visiting since Karen died," Mark said with the same sense of remorse.

"Well, what brings Steve back home?" Margie asked with a smile, trying to lighten the mood and change the subject.

"He just thought it would be nice to pay a visit and let his boy get to see Cedar Bluff," Mark replied, purposely not letting his friends in on Steve's latest trials with Charlie. "I don't have much in the frig, so thought I'd better stock up."

"Charlie, isn't it, Steve's boy?" Margie inquired.

"Must be twelve years old by now," Buster said.

"Thirteen I think," Mark said with a puzzled look, not quite sure himself.

"Aww…thirteen years old. You better stock up for sure. Teenage boy will probably eat you out of house and home, c'mon I'll help you find some things a growing boy might enjoy," Margie said with a warm, helpful smile, noticing how nervous Mark seemed about having to entertain at his home.

Mark was a bachelor. He didn't know where to begin when it came to preparing to have a kid at his house, and the thought of entertaining a teenager for the whole summer was beginning to hit him.

When he left the store, he felt a bit better. Margie had helped him get what he needed. Margie and her husband, Bill, had raised their two children and now had grandchildren Charlie's age. He would certainly keep her in mind to help him out later if needed. She wouldn't mind and would probably love to be involved.

As Mark drove toward home, he thought about Steve. His wife, Karen, had grown up in Cedar Bluff. Everyone had loved her. She was kind, generous, and always had a smile for anyone she encountered. Steve had been that way once. The two had made the perfect couple. The handsome star of the football team and the beautiful track star. Both were smart. Both were motivated. But both preferred the big city. Minneapolis called to them both.

Mark would need to prepare himself and his house. In a couple days, Steve and Charlie would be here, and he wasn't quite sure how the mood would be when they arrived.

CHAPTER 7

CHARLIE AT UNCLE MARK'S

"I can't believe my dad thinks this is somehow going to be good for me," I thought to myself as I sat down for dinner with my dad and his brother, Uncle Mark.

Looking around the kitchen, I could tell that decorating wasn't Mark's area of expertise. His house definitely was old, but pretty big for a guy living by himself. Most of the walls consisted of dark paneling. In spots, the sheets of paneling were pushing out at the seams, and the rusty nail heads were exposed. The rest of the walls were white paint, badly in need of some touch up or a fresh coat of paint. Upon arrival, I got the tour of the place. The house was an old two story farmhouse, nearly a perfect square except for the piece sticking out the back that acted as a porch. The porch was also the main entrance of the house, connecting to the kitchen. On the main floor, there was a living room, a bathroom, a dining room, and a kitchen. The upstairs consisted of two bedrooms and a bathroom. All the rooms were pretty good size, but the dimensions of the house were fairly small. I only got a quick peek at Mark's bedroom. It looked pretty cluttered with lots of clothes laying everywhere. I could tell Mark was a little embarrassed. The rest of the house was very clean, very organized. It was obvious that Mark had concentrated his cleaning efforts on the rest of the house, probably when he found out about our impending visit.

What was to be my bedroom for the next couple of months was actually not that bad, probably a 14 foot by 14 foot bedroom. Not as big as my room back home, but pretty nice. I especially liked the view out the windows, one on the left wall as you came in, and one straight ahead. My room was a corner room, and when I looked outside I could see a field that ran for about 100 yards, until it ended at some woods that looked like it continued up a wooded hill. The other window had a view of the field continuing up the valley. The bed was small and was shoved in the corner between the two windows. Not a thing on the walls. It was simple, but I didn't mind simple and plain. Mark had explained that he had borrowed a dresser; he didn't say where it was.

"Charlie," Mark held out a plate of hamburgers at dinner, nodding his head as an invitation to take another.

As I squirted some ketchup on my burger, my father and uncle laid out the game plan that I was going to follow for the next three months. Mark had given that whole secret away as soon as we arrived and I saw my dad cringe. What my dad had told me would be a week or two had suddenly turned into the whole summer. I had started to protest, but thought better of it. Fighting it would have to wait. Mark was too busy pretending to look excited about the whole thing.

"I really appreciate you being willing to watch Charlie this summer," my father said.

Without looking up from his plate, Mark replied, "Well..like I said, it'll be a busy summer, and I could certainly use the help."

Clearly for my benefit my father then said, "So, what are some things you need Charlie to do for you this summer?"

"He can help out around the house and help me with new things I got going. Nothing too difficult," Mark said the last sentence, looking right at me.

I wasn't sure if Mark thought I was incompetent or something. I'm sure my father had clued him in on the stuff with the police back home. Maybe he had told Mark about some of my habits.

"I guess we haven't talked much lately," my dad continued, "How is the job going, sanding wood floors, right?"

Mark nodded as he swallowed his burger, "Yeah, I was only sanding people's wood floors and refinishing them. But, everyone's going to laminate floors lately. So, I work for a place in La Crosse quite a bit...a flooring place. They call me when someone buys some laminate, and I install it. Hardwood floors as well."

"How's that going?" My dad asked, always interested in hearing about an entrepreneurial venture.

"Good. Started slow, but now it's darn near five days a week, plus some weekends. So, as you can see," Mark said with a wave of his arm, "housekeeping doesn't always come first. Also, my chores around my little farm here sometimes get behind."

"Well, Charlie here will help you with anything you need this summer," My dad said with a smile, then looking at me, "won't you Charlie?"

"Yeah," is all I managed to say, not looking up.

"What do I know about farms?" I thought to myself. "I didn't realize Mark would be off working all day long. Was I supposed to stay here in the old farmhouse all day long and take care of things?"

"So, you mentioned some new things you have going," my dad continued to pound Mark with questions, maybe trying to get me interested more than anything, "What type of new things?"

"You'll have to wait and see," Mark said, finally showing more excitement than nervousness, "I'll show you tomorrow. We should get the dishes cleaned up and get ready for bed soon."

Bed? I looked at the old clock on Mark's wall. It was barely 9:00 p.m. We had been at Mark's house for less than three hours, and the guy wanted to go to bed already. Back home, I wouldn't be sneaking out for at least another two hours.

"Wash or dry?" Mark asked as we got up from the table and he and my dad started clearing the table.

"Huh?" I said, a little stunned.

"Wash or dry?" Mark said again, pausing and looking right at me.

When I didn't say anything right away, Mark answered for me.

"You can wash, Charlie, I'll dry. That will give your
dad a chance to sit and relax after a long day of driving."
Mark motioned for me to follow him as he and my dad
gathered the plates and headed into the kitchen.

"Charlie doesn't get a chance to do too many dishes.
Jane, our housekeeper, takes good care of us. But, I think
it's a great opportunity for Charlie to take on some
responsibility while he's here," my dad said to Mark as if I
wasn't there.

Mark right away began filling the sink and putting in
some dish soap. He opened a drawer, pulled out a towel
and tossed it to me. Mark began putting plates, utensils,
and plastic cups into the hot water in the sink.

"Start scrubbin'," Mark said, with a smile and turned
his attention to his brother, who took a seat at the small
kitchen table.

As my dad and Mark talked about how the hot,
summer weather had arrived earlier than normal, and what
businesses are still in town, I began to wipe the food off the
dishes. I took two swipes at a plate with a dish clothe, then
reached into the drawer where I had seen Mark pull out a
towel, and pulled one out. I quickly dried my hands with it
and put it on the counter next to the sink. Then I dabbed
some more at the plate, then put it back in the water and
dried my hands again with the towel. Again I fished in the
sink for a plate. This time I tried to wash off the entire
plate before putting it in the adjoining sink, but couldn't
resist the temptation to release it back into the water and
grab the dry towel. Mark turned his attention away from

his brother and their conversation long enough to notice
my apprehension.

"What's wrong? Water too hot?" Mark jabbed his
hand into the water and declared it just fine. He gave me a
puzzled look and turned his attention back to my father.

I made another attempt. This time finished a plate, but
in my haste to clean off a plate in one fair swoop, some
ketchup got on the back of my thumb. Quickly, I grabbed
for the towel on the counter and wiped it off. I was
starting to not feel that good. I knew that I was in danger
of giving away my biggest secret, my biggest
embarrassment, the fear of having my hands dirty. Neither
my father nor Mark were paying attention, still discussing
the folks in Cedar Bluff, Mark drying the lone dish I had
managed to wash. I reached into the water again bravely
this time pulling out a fork. I quickly tried to scrub the
food off with the dish cloth, feeling slightly dizzy. My face
was feeling hot. Nervously, I dropped the fork back into
the water and grabbed for the towel, but stopped short.
The ketchup from the plate was clearly visible on the towel.
I again reached in the drawer for a fresh one.

"What's the problem?" Mark asked, his attention now
on me, looking at the towels on the counter and the empty
sink in front of him.

"Are you O.K.?" My dad now asked, noticing the
beads of sweat mounting on my forehead. "Here, let me
help you out," my dad said as he took his spot at the sink.

I relinquished the dish cloth and sat on the chair my
dad had just vacated.

"Looks like it was a long ride for you too," Mark said, looking a bit concerned.

"I'm alright," I had managed to say, "Just not feeling too good, mind if I go lie down?"

"Yeah, head to the living room," Mark replied, "We'll take care of the dishes tonight.

I made a beeline to the bathroom to wash my hands before lying down on the couch. I felt nauseous, but wasn't sure if it was getting my hands dirty, fear of my dad and Uncle Mark noticing my issues with doing the dishes, or being in the strange house with so many things in an unorganized fashion. I needed structure and cleanliness to feel normal. After a while, I decided that sleep was what I needed and excused myself to my new bedroom. As I lay down in bed, my new "temporary bedroom" in his uncle's house in Cedar Bluff, Minnesota, I felt grateful that I was tired, so I could fall asleep fast.

CHAPTER 8

CHARLIE – THE FARM

The next morning I awoke to my father sitting on the edge of my bed with his hand on my forehead.

"Just checking to see if you have a fever," he told me. "You had us a bit worried last night."

"Just tired," I said, sitting up in bed and getting my bearings.

"Come on downstairs for breakfast, then get cleaned up, we'll check out Mark's farm, then go to town. I need to pick up some things for you...for your stay with Mark."

"O.K.," I said quietly.

The wood floor was cold on my feet. I searched for my socks and pants and then headed down the stairs. All the floors in the old farmhouse were without carpet, wood flooring that was smooth under my socks.

I didn't mind Mark's cooking, chunky hash browns, bacon, and orange juice. Back home, Jane was more about fruit and less about bacon. There was nothing wrong with fresh fruit, but I sort of felt like one of the guys sitting around the kitchen table with my dad and Uncle Mark eating greasy food.

"Feeling better?" Mark asked.

"A little," I said. Truth was, I felt good, but I didn't want to be the one doing dishes. Luckily, my dad volunteered again to handle the dishes, so I was off the hook.

After a hot shower, we went outside to explore the farm, as my dad put it. He seemed happier than I've seen him in a long time. I could tell he really liked being back in Cedar Bluff, and having a chance to hang around with Mark. I began to wonder why our visits to Cedar Bluff had become so sparse. We first went to the old barn. It looked really old. But it looked solid. Huge beams supported the walls and the rafters. I followed behind as my father and Mark talked. The air in the barn smelled stale, but I could also make out the smell of freshly cut wood, which smelled sort of nice.

"I've been looking forward to having you see my place, since I bought it last fall," Mark explained to us. "This barn, like the house is pretty old. This barn was built in 1908, along with the house. But Winnebago Creek took the house in 1941, so the house is newer, if you can call nearly 70 years old newer."

When Mark told us he'd been hoping we would visit earlier, when he first bought the place, I saw my dad hang his head a bit. I could tell my dad felt bad about not staying in touch with his brother.

"Looks like it was mainly used for horses, judging by the stalls....and hay above," My dad observed, trying to regain his composure.

"Yeah, outside I'll show you where the old cow barn was. Previous owner gave up milking and took down the barn to add more crops once milk prices took a dive few years back," Mark said, and my dad shook his head, as if he knew about milk prices.

On the way out of the barn, Mark picked up his pace. I tried hard to match his long strides. He talked as he went.

"Over there," Mark said, pointing to nothing but corn "Is where the cow barn stood before the creek got her. Let's head up the valley, I'll show ya the upper valley and what I got goin' up there."

We walked along a dirt road, which looked like it was only used for tractors. We were surrounded by bluffs on each side with corn in the middle. To my left, only 30 feet away I could hear the creek, hidden by vegetation, flowing back down the valley. I couldn't tell how wide it was…10 feet, 20 feet maybe. The tall weeds and small trees hid the creek and its dimensions like a whispering secret. Just beyond the other bank, the bluff rose nearly straight up, its height also hidden by overhanging trees near us, protected from view by the bright sun just now shining over the top of the bluff. To the right, corn stretched only a hundred yards or so, until it too ended at a steep bluff. Straight ahead of us was what looked like a dead end valley with corn ending at a gentle slope, then climbing steeper into the hills. I found myself falling behind Mark and my father, too busy absorbing the views to match their pace.

Finally we stopped at the end of the corn. In front of us were over 100 small trees. Beyond the small trees, all planted in rows, was a brushy slope that became all forest as the hill quickly steepened. Over half of the small trees sat low in the valley before beginning to gain elevation.

"Charlie, do you know what those are?" Mark asked, waiting for me to catch up, then taking a quick glance at my father.

"I don't know," I said, shrugging.

"Apple trees," My father said with a smile.

"Apple trees," Mark echoed with a grin.

"That's your little surprise," My dad said rather than asked.

"Yeah. Planted them last fall. They were only five feet high when I bought them from Bluffside Orchard. They've already picked up a foot or so since then. Right now I'm leasing the crop land that holds the corn to the Dunn's down the valley a bit. Ronnie Dunn owns the rest of the way back in the valley, 120 acres of mostly woods and set aside. If I save my pennies, someday I'll buy it from him, he's getting pretty old and none of his kids live around here anymore. Then I'd put it all in apple trees….start my own orchard." Mark told us with excitement masking disappointment.

"You'll pull it off," My dad said confidently, probably seeing in Mark's face the same thing I saw….some goals take a long time and a lot of work to reach.

"I worry about the lower part of the orchard. The ground stands not much higher than the creek." Mark said, taking a moment to scan the young apple trees and the valley above before turning toward us and motioning us to follow.

"Yeah, but it's just this section of the field that sits so low," my dad replied reassuringly.

"Only takes one weak spot to flood a valley. C'mon, I'll show you where my property goes up the hill," Mark said as he made his way to a thick row of saplings.

"How old is that bridge?" My dad asked, pointing about a quarter mile ahead.

Looking in that direction, I could see the top of what looked to be a metal structure, just visible above some small trees.

"Pretty old. The loggers put it in quite some ago when they were logging off the hillside." Mark said. "It's not really much of a road across there, more or less a logging road used by tractors and skidders."

We followed Mark away from the apple trees and toward some small trees across the dirt road. The vegetation looked almost impenetrable until I saw where Mark was heading. A narrow trail snuck through the trees and dropped down a steep slope to the edge of a shallow creek.

"Winnebago Creek?" My dad asked.

"Yep, this is the Winnebago." Mark replied turning around. "It's up a bit from some recent rains, but it can really draw down, especially in late summer. But, it can be a dangerous little flow, can fill up just like that after a big rain," Mark said as he snapped his fingers.

"Let's cross the creek, then we can head up the hill, catch the logging road, that'll take us back home," Mark said as he began walking upstream to a couple downed trees stretching over the water.

I looked at the jumble of tree trunks and branches just ahead of me as I walked toward it, and immediately had my doubts. I couldn't see how anybody could use that as a bridge. Looking across the creek, probably about 25 feet across, I saw that the bank on the other side of the creek was steep from years of high, fast water scouring away the soil on the side of the creek that that held the hill, going up at a 45 degree angle from the water's edge. Many trees lay in the water or partially in the water on that side, trees that had lost their earth footing during the spring floods. The mess of timber that lay across the creek had experienced that similar fate, not having enough foot hold for the roots and had tumbled across the creek. By the looks of it, a larger tree had fell over, taking a white birch with it as it fell.

"We could go upstream a ways to the old bridge, but this is quicker," Mark said pointing at the jumble of logs lying across the creek.

"Do you use this crossing instead of the bridge much?" my dad asked, looking a bit uncertain.

"I've crossed the creek on these downed trees a few times while turkey hunting," Mark said as he gained a foot hold on the trunk of the biggest down tree, "Go slow and use the branches as hand holds and it's not a problem."

Mark led the way across the fallen trees, his boots carefully using both trees to pick his way along, grabbing branches with his hands to keep himself upright. My dad followed along and soon both were standing on the opposite bank, waiting for me.

"See, Charlie, just take your time and hold onto some of the upright branches to steady yourself, and it's easy," my dad said trying to reassure me.

I started out just as I had seen them do. My sneakers searched for footing on the slippery logs, by hands seeking out branches as I kept my head down watching my every step. Soon I was out over the water. The logs started out only a foot or so above the water, which was only a foot or so deep by the looks of it, but the logs increased in elevation as they traveled to the higher, steeper bank across the creek. I was about half way across, with Mark and my dad constantly saying, "slowly", "take your time", and "watch your step", when my foot slipped off the bigger log. My first instinct was to grab a branch with both hands. My weight made me swing a bit until my back was out over the pointy branches of the smaller birch tree. Pulling upward as hard as I could, I was able to pull myself upright, but not without pushing off a wet, dirty log with my left hand. When I was again standing straight and had found my balance, I looked at my hand. Dirt and little pieces of wood were mixed with moisture on my palm and fingers. Without thinking, I knelt on the log to lean down into the water, two feet below to rinse it off.

"What are you doing!" Mark shouted. "Stand up!"

"Charlie!" yelled out my dad.

I stretched as far as I could and was unable to touch the water with my dirty hand. Then, just like that, my left foot slipped off the log and my foot shot down below the log. My hand was unable to touch the water, but my foot managed. My sneaker splashed into the water up to my calf.

"Pull yourself up!" One of the guys on the bank yelled.

Embarrassed, I was able to again pull myself to my feet.

"What were you doing?" Mark questioned with annoyance when, for the second time, I stood upright.

I shrugged my shoulders thinking of a rational excuse for suddenly having the need to water off my hand, "I needed to get the dirt off my hands.....for grip," I managed to respond.

"Well, come on across and be more careful this time," Mark told me.

I soon made it to the other side, without any other mishaps, and my uncle and dad grabbed my arms to help me the final couple steps.

"Don't cross too many logs in Minneapolis, huh?" Mark said with a chuckle.

"No," I said with a small smile, feeling my face redden.

Turning to head up the hill, Mark said, "Follow me. It's a little steep. But it's only a ways until the logging road....and use the trees as hand holds to pull yourself uphill," Mark said.

Following behind, I could see a faint trail through the brush and small trees. It was early June, and the woods were thick and the bugs were bad as we tagged along with Mark, my wet foot squishing in my shoe. Mark's long stride and powerful legs pulled himself up the hill with ease. It wasn't long before both my dad and I were breathing hard.

"Let's stop and let Charlie catch his breath," My dad said to Mark, probably as much to my father's benefit as mine.

"Sure," Mark said, and came down the hill a few steps to join us.

I tried not to show my fatigue and my dad, who was all into conversation earlier, was now quiet, breathing deeply and rapidly in and out. We were now at a higher elevation and Mark pointed out over the fields below.

"The trees are pretty dense, but you can sort of make out the size of the corn field that makes up my land that Dunn leases," Mark said pointing through the trees.

We only nodded and looked, still panting. The view was obscured, but still pretty cool. Through the leaves, I could just make out the corn field, rising up the hill on the other side of the narrow valley, stopping at the woods and bluff across from us, only a couple hundred yards away. Up the valley farther, I could see the old metal bridge Mark was talking about. It didn't look like much.

"Well, let's go, only about 40 yards to the logging road, and then it flattens out," said Mark and he began to head uphill.

Minutes later, we were standing on the logging road. The road was nothing more than a flat trail about 10 feet wide carved out of the side of the hill. The uphill side of the road, like the creek below, a steep bank, three to four feet high created by some earth moving machine that had dug into the bluff to create the road.

"Previous owner put this in thirty some years ago when he logged off some of his land," Mark said noticing where I was looking. "Came up with a dozer and cleared a path to bring in the logs. I think the bridge across the creek was in long before that. This logging road will cross that bridge upstream."

"The southwest corner of my property is right over there," Mark said pointed up the road and uphill. There's a fence just a ways uphill from here, can't see it with all the trees. The fence running uphill to meet the corner of my land is down in places, but you can see it right over there where it would cross the logging road."

I could see a barbed wire fence attached to metal posts on either side of the logging road, allowing the road to be open. Looking along the road uphill, I could see where the logging road crested the hill at an angle and disappeared over the top.

Mark continued, "To the right, beyond the fence is George Bulman's property. He has over 400 acres, and his farm is over the hill. If you follow the logging road over the top, you'll end up right behind his house. Nice guy... has a son your age I think Charlie. Maybe we'll walk the road to the Bulman's sometime."

"I remember the Bulman's," dad said with a remembering look. "Is George still raising horses?"

Mark nodded, "Yeah, but just as a hobby, even though he has some pricey mares. He has most of his money in corn and soy beans. My buddy Buster lives up the valley from him. Let's head downhill this way, and we'll come out right by my house."

The rest of the walk was easy....downhill. The logging road was full of brambles with thorns that grabbed your legs and scratched your hands, but at least it wasn't as exhausting as the climb up. Within ten minutes the logging road intersected with the creek. This time we could tell a gravelly path had been cleared in the creek for when vehicles wanted to cross the creek. We simply took off our shoes and walked across, water coming just over our ankles. The cool water felt good on our feet. I took a moment to wash my face and hands before stepping on the other bank and putting my shoes back on.

After lunch we drove into town. My dad wanted to drive around town since it had been a while since he was in town.

"Just to check out the town," my dad told me when he saw how uninterested I was at the prospect of checking out the puny town of Cedar Bluff.

I could tell my father was enjoying himself, which was the first time in a long time. Since my mom died, our visits to Cedar Bluff had been brief and my dad wasn't always in such a good mood. It seemed different this time.

As we drove down the gravel road to Cedar Bluff, Mark pointed out the different farms and houses to my dad and they talked about who lived there. Occasionally, we'd seen a fisherman standing on the bank of the creek or standing in the water in waders in spots where the trees didn't block out the view of the creek.

"Fishin' for brown trout," Mark said when he saw me watching a fisherman.

When we reached the main highway and rolled into town, it didn't take long to drive past a few landmarks or people's houses they knew, included Mark's old apartment, that he lived in up until just last fall.

After a quick lunch at The Fisherman's, a café on Main Street, we stopped at Harris' Grocery. My dad said he needed to pick up a few items that he thought I would need during my stay with Uncle Mark. It wasn't much of a supermarket. When we went inside, it was only a handful of aisles of groceries and one freezer for the whole place.

"Steve!" Margie Harris shouted when she saw my dad and ambled over to give him a big hug. "It's so good to see you!"

"Hi Margie. Hi Bill," My dad said when Margie released her grip and saw Margie's husband Bill walking down the short aisle from the counter to greet them.

"And look at Charlie!" Margie exclaimed. "I haven't seen you since you were a little boy, my how you've grown." She said turning her attention to me.

Apparently, Margie and Bill were the owners of the grocery store we had just entered. I instantly like Margie. She reminded me of Mrs. Claus as you see her in movies. She was a larger woman who seemed overly happy about seeing my dad and Uncle Mark.

Sensing my apprehension, Margie went for the handshake instead of a hug with me.

"Nice to meet to you Charlie," Margie said, extending her hand to me. I shook it, feeling my face begin to warm while everyone focused their attention on me.

"Charlie," Mr. Harris addressed me with much less exuberance than his wife and shook my hand as well. I shook his hand, looking down, and then wiped my hand on my pants.

A momentary silence fell upon the group, waiting for some sort of response from me.

"Well," said my dad, "we just have a few things to get for Charlie. Some shampoo and some lotion for the bug bites we picked up this morning hiking in the woods.

"Sure, we can help you out," said Margie. "Follow me."

We followed Margie as Bill went about his business unloading some boxes at the end of the aisle.

I could see the disappointment in my dad's face and a hint of uncertainty in Uncle Marks. I could have said something to these nice people and didn't. Once again, I looked like a jerk.

CHAPTER 9

CHARLIE – ALONE ON THE FARM

When I first got to Uncle Mark's I couldn't wait for my dad to leave. His enthusiasm was beginning to bother me. Besides, I think he was just trying to get me excited to be here. But, when Mark and my dad were carrying out the bags to leave and my dad was thanking Mark and telling him how much help I'd be, I began to worry. What if I didn't know what to do around the farm while Mark was working? What if Mark got mad at me? What if I couldn't stand being surrounded by bluffs and living in some old house? Mostly, I worried about Mark finding out about my quirks. I could see him calling my dad and saying, "Come get your weirdo son!"

Suddenly I felt a nervous sickness come over me. Suddenly I was angry at my dad for dumping me in some little hick town to spend my summer staring at cornfields and whatever stupid tasks Mark had planned for me.

"Charlie," my dad said putting his hands on both of my shoulders," This will be a good thing for you. You'll have a great summer here."

As my dad gave me a hug, my anger wouldn't let me hug back. It was just like it's been for the past few years.

He was going to go back to work and leave me with someone else. Except instead of our housekeeper, he was leaving me with his brother. Great. Thanks Dad.

"I'll call you often," he said and loosened his grip on me.

I felt it was a no win deal for me. As I walked back into the house, I could hear Mark say, "Don't worry Steve, we'll be O.K. here."

Sitting in my new bedroom, I heard my dad drive off. Moments later Mark tapped lightly on the bedroom door and came in.

"Look," Mark began, and sat down next to me on the bed, you're mad at your dad, I understand that, but...." Mark paused, choosing his words carefully, "You're here, and I'm glad. Consider this summer a chance to help out your good old uncle here." Mark chuckled, jabbing his thumb in his own chest, "I could use it."

Mark grabbed me playfully on the back of my neck and said, "Come on downstairs, I'll make some lunch in a while."

"I'll be down a little later," I said, forcing a smile as Mark left the room.

If I was going to be here all summer, I would need to rearrange my room, or I'd go nuts.

In less than an hour, I had emptied my suitcases out and put everything in my closet. Mark had offered to empty out and bring in the dresser he had been using, but I declined, instead asked for two chairs. Mark looked at me kind of funny, but obliged, hauling up two wooden chairs from the dining room. My room now had a bed, centered along the wall, with a chair on each side against the same wall. The dresser would have thrown off my symmetry. My clothes went in the closet. I think that's why I love swimming so much. It's such a symmetrical sport. Five strokes, breathe to the right, five strokes breathe to the left, and so on. Besides, it's pretty hard to feel dirty when swimming with the water rushing past you. I went downstairs for lunch feeling a bit better.

During lunch, Mark spelled out the plan for me.

"I'm not going to try to work you into the ground," Mark said with a smile. "Don't worry about that. I have some outdoor things to get accomplished, and some indoor projects. You get to choose what days you do what."

Mark paused and waited for me to respond in some way. I gave a little shrug as if to say O.K., but I think he interpreted it to be a shrug saying, "Do I have a choice."

Mark continued, "Now, it's not like you just have to spend your day working for me. This coming weekend is our city celebration, Mayfly Days, it's….." Seeing my puzzled look, Mark explained, "A mayfly is an insect, like a fly with big wings that hatches up off the bottom of the river with his buddies all on one night, and flies around. Makes a mess. Attracted to light. You should see the gas station. They pile up and die next to the pumps. Anyway, there's a big citywide celebration at our Community Center. It's a big party really. I'll introduce you to some good kids. You'll have a chance to get together with some boys this summer. You'll have fun."

"All right," I said. I was a bit uncertain about who Mark would introduce me to. When he said he'd introduce me to some "good" kids, it made me think about some of the geeks from my school. Boring kids probably. Or, maybe he meant kids that don't break into warehouses.

After lunch Mark led me down the dirt road again, carrying a step ladder, to show me what my outdoor activities would consist of.

We came to the end of the corn field where the terrain began to rise up into the dead end valley.

"You're going to help me with some pruning of my apple trees," Mark told me and waved his arm at his trees, leaning the ladder against a fence post. "It won't be hard work for you, and actually, you'll be outside, might be kinda nice," Mark told me with a smile, trying to convince me.

"What do I do?" I asked.

"Watch, I'll show you," Mark stepped to an apple tree and began teaching me how to prune.

"We're not trying to control the height or structure of the tree. We're trying to make a better quality apple by giving the young apples a chance to grow," Mark informed me as he took a big scissors like tool out of his pocket.

The trees had little apples beginning to form on the branches. Mark showed me where the basal cluster was on the branches. These were the part of the branch where new leaves formed at the same spot, sort of growing off from the same space. He showed me how to cut the new growth off at an angle using the big scissors he called a secateur.

"Pruning is an ongoing process," Mark continued. "As the summer goes by, we begin to remove any apples that have holes in them from worms or bugs, AND removing any apples that begin to touch one another. Apples need space to grow….to produce a quality fruit. If we take some out and leave space for others, we'll hopefully get some great apples by fall. What do you think? Can you handle it?" Mark asked.

"Yeah, sounds easy," I said with a smile.

I was serious. It didn't look too tough. There were parts of the trees that I couldn't reach, but could use the ladder. None of the trees were very high, so I would never have to get too far off the ground.

Back at the house, Mark showed me project number two. We stood in the dining room where we ate dinner two nights ago with my father.

"I have an old house," Mark said blankly. But, that doesn't mean it has to look old, at least inside. If possible, I'd like to paint it a brighter color, give it some life."

Turning to me Mark asked, "Have you ever done any painting?"

"No," I answered.

"Well," Mark said with a thoughtful look, "Maybe this is one project we tackle together. What do you think?"

"Sure, why not," The job didn't look too tough. It's not like there were too many things we'd have to pull off the walls. Actually, there wasn't anything to take off the walls except the outlet covers.

The next morning was Monday and Mark left early for work. He had told me that he had to work today, then Tuesday was an off day, apparently nobody needed to have floors put in. Then Wednesday through Friday were work days for him. I got out of bed and went downstairs. I looked at the clock and saw that it was nearly 8:00 a.m., which was early for me in the summer. But, I had heard Mark leave around 6:30, and I didn't have much luck getting back to sleep. Mark had gone shopping and told me he stocked up on food I might like. I found a box of Wheaties and poured myself a bowl. I was actually in a hurry to get started on the apple trees. Not that I relished the work, but it was so quiet in Mark's house that it was unnerving. It was a pretty big house, at least for a guy living alone, but it had such an old feeling that I felt claustrophobic. I was certainly used to living in a bigger house. My house back in Minneapolis was four times bigger than this one. And, Jane was always around, even if my father wasn't, so I was never really alone. Eating my cereal at the little kitchen table, I saw that Mark had left me a note along with the secateurs.

"Do what you can today. Have fun. Enjoy the day. Pizza in the freezer for lunch. Later! Mark." the note said.

I threw on a pair of shorts and a t-shirt, grabbed the secateurs and headed down the road toward the apple trees. I started at the first tree in the row closest to the road where Mark had left the ladder, the same tree Mark demonstrated on yesterday. I began searching for the clusters of leaves Mark told me about. I began trimming. It wasn't too hard until I had to use the ladder to reach a little higher. With all the branches coming off the little tree, I had trouble positioning the ladder. At first I tried opening up the ladder, but the ground wasn't level and the legs of the ladder sunk into the soft ground. I was only on the second step of the ladder when it began to tip over. I had to lean the closed ladder against the tree and find a gap in the branches to get a solid rest. Then I still had to reach around branches to get to the clusters.

By the second tree, nearly an hour later, the sweat was beginning to roll off me, burning my eyes, and my shoulders ached from reaching above my head. By the third tree a blister began forming on my thumb from using the secateurs. I made a goal to get four trees done and stop for lunch. I was only able to do that by switching the pruning tool to my left hand.

Back at the house, I popped a pizza into the oven and went about searching bathroom drawers for Band-Aids. Eating lunch, I couldn't help thinking that if this is how every day is going to be this summer, I'm in big trouble. I wish Mark had gone ahead and picked out the paint. I would have started painting the dining room just to get out of the sun.

I wasn't in any hurry to get back to my trees. Instead of starting where I'd left off, I walked up the hill past the row of apple trees. Coming to the end of the last row, I paused to look beyond the apple trees. The land was fairly open for nearly another 100 yards. A fence marked the end of the apple trees, the end of Mark's property. The rest was Ronnie Dunn's. Tall grass, brush, and little trees grew up and I could see paths carved out of the brush, probably deer or something. Looking to my right, I saw some movement along the apple trees only about 60 yards away. Through the leaves and branches of the trees, something brown was moving. A deer suddenly came into view. It was eating off one of the apple trees. That was the first time I had seen a deer in the wild, except for the ones that you see while driving. I watched it for several minutes. It didn't make a sound as it nosed the branches of the tree eating. After a minute or so, it walked directly away from me along the apple trees and disappeared into the forest on the far side of the stand of apple trees. Suddenly, I was aware of my breathing, which was rapid. My heart was pounding in my chest as if I had been running. That was pretty cool I thought as I turned to walk back downhill to my row of trees where I left off.

Two hours later I had had enough. My shoulders ached, the blister on my hand was only partially protected by the Band-Aid, which kept coming off my sweaty thumb, and I was exhausted. It was only three o'clock, but I began to consider heading back to the house. But, I was curious. The woods where the deer had vanished earlier, was about 75 yards way. I thought I would take a look to see what the woods looked like on that side of the narrow valley. I began heading that way, walking between the last rows of corn, still only a foot high in mid-June, and the first row of apple trees. I reached the woods and saw that it resembled the woods along the creek, tightly choked with brush and small trees along the field edge, except for chosen spots where narrow trails were carved. Ducking to clear some low hanging branches, I squeezed through one of the gaps, the one where I thought I had seen the deer enter. Looking down, I could see the deer's tracks, indented into the soft earth, the grass and weeds gone, victim of deer and other animals crossing. I stepped over a log to go down an incline into a small ravine, a dry creek bed probably, when I felt something sharp against my leg.

"Ow!" I said aloud, instinctively slapping at my leg.

Before I knew it, the stinging feeling grew on my legs. Then I heard them. I was straddling a tree, under which was a ground hive of hornets.

"Aww!" I screamed and sprinted back into the field. I kept running as fast as I could. The burning in my legs was excruciating. I ran toward home but felt the hornets around me still. Instead of taking the left turn around the corner of the corn and down the dirt road back to the house, I made a beeline straight for the creek. Ducking to make it through the brush and trees, I leaped into the water and sat down in the cold creek. Fearing that the hornets had followed me, I laid back in the shallow water, submerging every inch of me. I held my breath for the count of ten, then lifted my head up and had a look around. I had managed to outrun the hornets, but running my hands along my legs under the water, realized that I had been stung a dozen or so times, even one nasty one inside my shorts on my upper thigh.

The road back to the house seemed longer than usual. Again, I searched through the drawers in the bathroom and again was lucky enough to find some cream to put on my stings. I even added some to the back of my neck where I realized I had a painful sunburn. I changed clothes, grabbed a glass of ice water and lay down on the couch to rest, thankful to have a little time before Mark came home.

CHAPTER 10

MARK

"Charlie, Charlie," Mark said when he got home from work and found his nephew asleep on the couch.

At first, Mark had thought, he's spent the entire day laying around the house, but then he saw the white blotches of calamine lotion on his sunburned legs, and knew right away he'd given it a go with my apple trees.

"Looks like you tangled with some hornets," Mark said and couldn't help chuckling a little bit.

"Yeah, hurts still," Charlie said, grimacing and scratching his legs.

"Well, you look a mess! I saw a water trail coming up the porch steps and into the kitchen too. What happened?" Mark asked Charlie, sitting down in a chair across from the couch.

Charlie filled him in. They both had to laugh a bit when Charlie told how he jumped in Winnebago Creek to escape the hornets.

"There certainly were some low points to your day," Mark told Charlie. "Hornets and sunburn, sounds like a fun day at work," Mark said with heavy sarcasm.

"That's not the end of it," Charlie said, sitting up on the couch and holding out his hands, revealing his blisters.

"Eww," Mark said with a grimace. "That's my fault. I should have given you some gloves. I forgot. You still have city hands."

"How did the pruning go?" Mark asked.

"Four trees," Charlie said, "It wasn't too bad all considering. Oh, and I saw a deer!" Charlie exclaimed. "It didn't even know I was there! It was eating the apple trees, I watched for a while, but then it just walked off."

"Sounds like an eventful day!" Mark said with a chuckle. "Let's get some more ointment on your sunburn and those stings. Then I'll grill some steaks for us. You can chill out; sit on the porch while I grill. You must have been sleeping pretty hard. I found a couple pies on the porch. Note said 'From Margie Harris', she may have knocked, but you must not have heard."

Charlie ate like a horse. We had some big steaks and potatoes and carrots cooked in tinfoil packets thrown on the grill. The pies were great. Mark should have known Margie would take it upon herself to pitch in and help him out. Good old Margie.

Mark had been worried about Charlie all day and hesitated to call him while he worked. Steve had told him about Charlie's attitude problems, his run in with the law, and how he seemed angry at everyone around him. They agreed that Charlie needed to be given some responsibility. With some luck maybe he'd develop some sort of work ethic. They also debated how much space to give Charlie. Space to find some of these things himself. The first day seemed like a mess, but Mark could tell from the excitement in his voice that it wasn't all a disaster.

"Charlie," Mark began to say while they carried the plates from the porch to the kitchen.

"Yeah," Charlie answered.

"I have tomorrow off. I thought maybe we could go fishing. What do you think?" Mark inquired.

"Sure, I guess," was Charlie's reply.

Charlie didn't sound too sure, but Mark figured he'd push his luck some more.

"Mind if I bring along a guest?" Mark asked, hoping for a more enthusiastic response.

"A guest?" Charlie said.

"My friend Dianna. She's a pediatrician. She lives in Minneapolis. We've been seeing each other for two years now. Kinda tough because she lives and works there and I'm here. But, she's nice, you'll like her," Mark informed Charlie.

"Yeah, sure, that's cool," Charlie said. "I didn't know you had a girlfriend."

"Well, you and I probably haven't talked much lately, so I it never came up," Mark said. "Anyway, she'll roll in late tonight. You can meet her in the morning. She's a much better cook than I am, so I'm sure we'll have ourselves a feast tomorrow for breakfast. Then we'll go fishing, maybe pack a picnic lunch. Sound good?"

"Yeah, good," Charlie said.

After Charlie had gone to bed and Mark cleaned up his house a bit for Dianna's arrival, Mark couldn't help thinking that Charlie put forth a pretty good effort his first day all considering. Aside from some sunburn, blisters, hornet bites, and a little pain in his muscles, the kid did pretty good.

CHAPTER 11

CHARLIE - FISHING AND DIANNA

Even with a bad case of sunburn on my neck and some terrible hornet stings, I slept like a rock. After a big meal I could barely keep my eyes open much past dinner. Mark had dumped a ton of ointment on the stings and slathered my neck with aloe so when I woke up things were not quite so painful.

When I woke up, however, I began to worry. While I was in a haze, half asleep sitting on the couch, watching TV with Mark, he had told me that he was wasn't working tomorrow for sure, and that he planned to take me trout fishing. I barely remember him telling me until now. I had said, "Yeah, sure," but now I was I wasn't so sure. Brian had taken me fishing a bunch of times back home, but I didn't handle the actual fishing pole but only a couple times. I didn't want to look too inept in front of Mark. He was a lot like my father in many aspects. Neither felt the need to say too much to me, but obviously for different reasons. My father was usually too busy to talk to me. Mark, on the other hand, his reason for being selective in what he said to me I think was out of nervousness. I could tell he was used to having the place to himself. Then I remembered Mark's other bit of information, which came as a bit of a surprise. Apparently, Mark has a girlfriend. Dianna. Mark had said that she would come in later. I never heard her arrive. I was so tired, I never heard her car pull up, which is hard to believe given how quiet it is at night out in the country.

Curiosity caused me to move quickly to get out of bed and begin throwing on some sweatpants. It was only 7:00 a.m., early for me, but since I've been at Mark's, I've actually been sleeping good and getting up earlier and earlier.

I heard voices as I came down the creaky old wooden steps, telling me that I wasn't the only early bird in the house.

"Charlie," Mark said with a smile as I came into the kitchen. "This is Dianna."

"Hi Charlie!" A thin, brown haired woman in her mid-thirties said, turning from the stove and waving a spatula at me and smiling.

"How're the stings...and the sunburn...and the blisters," Mark asked with a laugh.

I couldn't help smiling back, "Fine."

"Sit down Charlie," Dianna said over her shoulder. "I made an omelet and toast."

I took a seat next to Mark.

"I was just going to go up and wake you for breakfast," Mark said, still smiling.

"It'll be a little while yet," Dianna said, mixing some eggs in a small bowl. "So, Charlie, Mark says you get to stay with him for the summer. That sounds like fun."

"Yeah," I said, searching for more to say but not being able to find the words.

"I hear he had you out pruning his apple trees. Sounds like a lot of work," Dianna said, still prodding me for a little return conversation.

"Yeah, it was kinda hot out," I said.

"I heard the ground hornets seem to like you too," Dianna said, still smiling and beginning to sit down with a big pan of omelet.

"Yeah, the stings are better now," I said rubbing my legs through my sweats.

"Let's eat." said Mark.

We ate with Dianna and Mark doing all the talking. I tried to find a way to say more to Dianna, but for some reason I just couldn't find the words. That was always a big problem for me.

After breakfast I watched Mark get us ready to go fishing while Dianna packed a picnic lunch. Mark got three fish poles, a small net, and an old, beat up five gallon bucket to put the fish in. My job was to dig up some worms.

I went to where Mark told me, next to the corn just beyond his yard. I jabbed the shovel into the soft earth. The first shovel full of dirt exposed two worms right away. I was then able to use the sharp spade end of the shovel to scoop up the first worm and then deposit it into the coffee can that Mark gave me. But, when I went to scoop up the second worm, I accidently cut it in half with the spade. I wasn't sure if the worm would be any good then, so I flung it into the corn with the shovel to hide the evidence. My next shovel full of dirt came up empty, no worms. I slid to the left a little bit and tried again, using my foot to push the shovel deep. By now Mark and Dianna came outside to join me, holding the fishing gear and our cooler full of lunches. When I brought up the shovel of dirt a big fat night crawler could be seen halfway out of the dirt. Out of the corner of my eye I could see Mark waiting, standing patiently just behind and to the side of me. I tried to pry it loose from the packed dirt with the shovel, lightly jabbing at the dirt with my shovel.

"Just grab it, we need to get rolling," Mark said, still trying to sound patient.

Then I saw Mark glance at Dianna and said to me, "Bust up the dirt....here like this."

Mark stooped over the dirt and reached forward, grabbing hold of the dirt and breaking it apart with his hands. Instantly, nearly a dozen worms could be seen in the now loosened dirt. Mark quickly grabbed them and put them in the can.

Mark did the same with the other shovel-sized clump of dirt and as he stood up said, "Can't be afraid to get your hands dirty, especially when we're going fishin'. Let's go."

I felt embarrassed as we started up the same dirt road we walked with my dad, heading up the valley. I tried not to look at Dianna. I felt like some sort of sissy for not wanting to touch the worms.

We again came to the apple orchard, but kept going, walking parallel to the creek, still hidden by trees and other vegetation. I could hear the movement of the water against rocks. Dianna tried to strike up a conversation asking me about school. I could tell she was avoiding asking me about my friends. I told her about being part of the swim team and she shared stories about being a cross country runner in high school.

The farther up the valley we walked, the closer we came to the old bridge. As the dirt road we were on turned to cross the bridge, I could see that it was mainly a couple cement slabs on top of some metal beams stretching 30 feet or so from bank to bank. Some metal railings attached to the cement platform were all that made up the little bridge. Mark led us down a rocky embankment to a flat spot next to the water.

"This little road over the bridge connects to the logging road we walked the other day," Mark pointed out. "It's mostly for tractors and other logging equipment. You could take this road and get to the other side of the bluff if you had to."

I looked at the little dirt road crossing the old concrete bridge. It didn't look too strong. The road cut into the woods but seemed to turn and run parallel with the creek. Downstream from the bridge, the creek snaked through the woods, rippling through the rocks in a shallow course. But just upstream from the bridge, the water looked slower, almost seeming to pool up underneath.

"It's deeper over there, along the bank," Mark said pointing to another cement slab leaning into the water under the bridge.

"That old chunk of concrete used to be part of the bridge platform, but it fell in the water, so they replaced it long ago. The water scours out a hole along the wall. Trout like to lie in there," Mark continued. "I'll get you both rigged up and you can cast it just upstream of the hole and let her drift in."

Mark quickly, and thankfully, put a worm on my hook and handed me the pole. It had a hook and worm, with a lead weight about a foot above the hook. The reel was one of those with the little flip bar things. I had no idea how to cast it. But I couldn't let on that I didn't know what I was doing. I had seen Brian do it before back home and tried to remember. I moved the little bar to one side and the line dropped down to the ground. I quickly reeled it back up and tried again, this time holding the line with one hand. I reared back with the pole and 'Smack!' the line and lead weight slapped the water in front of me.

"Ever use this type of rod and reel before," Dianna asked me with a polite smile.

"No, not like this one," I said.

"Just like this," she said and demonstrated with her rod. The line arched in the air and landed in the water and I watched her line drift in the current toward the wall.

I mimicked her actions and watched with surprise, and relief, as my line sailed out into the water and plopped not too far from where Dianna's landed and it began to drift downstream.

"Turn the handle and the bail will close," Dianna instructed, "Reel up a little and we'll be able to stay a little ways apart and not get tangled," she said. "I guess Mark needs to take more time to show you things," she said, turning to look at Mark, standing behind us with a sheepish look.

Mark was the first one to catch a fish. He tried to take Dianna's cue by telling me how to know when I had a fish. I was to keep my line tight and feel a tap, tap on the line, then set the hook by pulling the rod tip up. Mark fought the fish patiently while Dianna slipped the little net underneath it in the water and held it up for me to see.

"Brown trout." Mark said with a victorious grin.

Mark and Dianna both then caught one. All three trout went into the pail that Mark brought along, half filled with water from the creek.

I was still waiting for my first bite, when Dianna announced that she was going to go upstream and fish another hole.

"She knows where she's going," Mark said. "She's been fishing with me here before."

Just then, I felt a tapping on my line. I held my breath, waiting for one more tap. When it came I yanked the rod and reeled in fast, feeling no weight or fighting fish on the end.

"I had a bite," I said to Mark as we both stood side by side on the bank.

"You gotta take it easy," Mark said shaking his head. "Set the hook gentle, it doesn't take much, and if it isn't there, let it settle back in again and hopefully you'll get another chance."

"Sorry," I said.

Reeling the rest of the way in, I saw that my worm was gone.

"Cleaned you," Mark said. "Can you put another one on?"

"Sure," I said. But, I wasn't too sure.

I reached into the pail and pulled out a little worm. I had seen Brian hook on a worm a bunch of times. I knew what to do, but that didn't mean I wanted to do it. Quickly, I jabbed the hook into the worm once, then again. Blood and other juicy stuff oozed onto my fingers. I quickly set the rod down and crouched to wash off my hands. As I did, I saw the disgusted look Mark gave me. Instead of feeling embarrassed, I felt angry. Angry at Mark for looking at me like that, for putting me in this situation. Who said I wanted to go fishing anyway I thought. I angrily stood up, grabbed my rod, and flung a wild cast toward the hole. It landed on the other bank in the tall grass and I had to yank it hard to free it.

"Easy," Mark said.

"So," I said, feeling like getting back at Mark somehow, "How long have you had a girlfriend? Too bad you haven't called us to keep us informed," I said really snotty, loaded with sarcasm.

"What?" Mark replied with a baffled look.

"Just seems like you've been keeping secrets," I said, grasping for straws. Bad idea. Mark clearly didn't like hearing some griping from snotty teenagers.

"What are you talking secrets for?" Mark said, his voice becoming stern. "Have you ever asked your dad about his work, and more importantly how he is feeling? Have you checked on his well-being? You know, smart guy, you're not the only one who lost a loved one when your mom died? And…." Mark stopped, almost thinking about whether or not to say it, "What about all this hand washing and rearranging your room? You can't even greet anybody like a normal person. Make some eye contact! Act normal for Pete's Sake! Sounds like you have a few secrets of your own kiddo!"

I didn't know what to say. I was unable to look at Mark, ashamed.

"Look, sorry about that. We all have things about ourselves that we don't like, that worry us…that keep us up at night. But we can work through things. It's hard, but then we can stop worrying all the time," Mark said.

I didn't know what Mark meant by that, but then he continued.

"I'm sorry I didn't fill you in about every aspect of my life," Mark said, his tone softening. "Maybe we could both loosen up a bit."

We both then realized that Dianna was standing just upstream from us. She had come back and witnessed all the action.

"Sometimes a little help from friends and family can go a long way to conquering a fear," Dianna said with a smile.

CHAPTER 12

DIANNA

Dianna was a little surprised to hear that her boyfriend Mark had agreed to watch his nephew over the summer. For starters, Mark lived alone and liked to have his little farm to himself. He knew nothing about taking care of a teenager, especially one that had been in some trouble. Secondly, Mark had huge goals set for himself. He wanted to buy more land, grow apple trees, and be successful doing things on his own terms. Achieving those goals required hard work. Hard work means that Mark is not home that often, a fact that has made their two year relationship difficult at times. Luckily, being a physician can have long hours. Lucky because Dianna, living nearly three hours away from Mark, can keep herself busy, too busy to worry about whether this long distance relationship will work.

Mark had filled Dianna in about his brother Steve, Steve's wife dying, and how Steve had all but broken off contact with his hometown and brother, burying himself in his work. Mark also told her about Charlie, Steve's thirteen year old son, whose troubles finally reached a boiling point when he was charged with breaking and entering. Steve had nowhere else to turn. He had called Mark and Mark had agreed to watch Charlie for the summer, help the boy out and keep him away from the bad influences he was finding back home.

She wasn't worried about Mark being able to handle it though. Dianna had fallen in love with Mark because he was like her, driven and motivated to meet his goals, even if hard work and long hours were part of the equation. Like Mark, Dianna had never married. She was 36 years old and had dedicated her life to making it through medical school, then continuing the focus of being the best doctor she could be. Dianna felt that Mark would have excelled in college. He was driven enough, certainly intelligent enough. He could have done anything he wanted. But his goals were different. He didn't want to work for somebody else. He wanted to be his own boss. It was only a matter of time before he found a way to make it happen.

She was much more worried about Charlie. He had a lot of insecurities. When they met that morning in the kitchen, he didn't make any eye contact with her. Also, Mark keeps telling her about how he's obsessed with cleanliness and always washing his hands. She saw that first hand when he was digging for worms.

"The kid has a lot issues," she thought to herself as she packed her bag to head back to Minneapolis.

"Mark, it's really nice that you're watching Charlie for the summer," Dianna told Mark as they leaned against her car in front of the house. "You're good for him."

Mark sighed deeply. "I just wish he wasn't so…so…weird, you know, he has this way of interacting with people, it's just not normal."

"Maybe you can help him," Dianna said putting her hand on Mark's agitated shoulder.

"Yeah, I don't know what to do. He's been here less than a week and he's moving furniture around, he's paranoid about getting his hands dirty, and I'm embarrassed whenever I introduce him to anybody."

"Look Mark," Dianna pleaded. "I've known kids like Charlie. I've referred them to specialists. I think he has an obsessive compulsive disorder. The hand washing, the tidiness, the need for order in everything around him; all the signs are there."

Mark grimaced and shook his head. "Obsessive compulsive disorder? I've heard of it, but...seriously, do you think that's what's troubling this kid? What about the trouble he's gotten into back home? Is that part of it too?"

"I'm afraid that's a whole other issue," Dianna said.

With a deep sigh Mark said, "Well Doc, what can I do? How can I help him?"

"You're doing a lot of it already," Dianna said. "You're there for him. You've taken him in and gotten him away from some of the bad elements he's been hanging with back home. You've given your brother, and Charlie, a break from each other. Chances are Charlie acts out because he's mad at his dad. He's trying to find someone to blame for his mom dying. I don't know, maybe he's depressed on top of it all."

"Oh great," Mark said with heavy sarcasm, throwing his hands in the air. "Some compulsive disorder, behavior problems, AND depression!? We better stop this conversation before you diagnose him with some more stuff."

"I'm only trying to help," Dianna said softly.

"I know," Mark said wrapping his big arms around Dianna. "I appreciate you letting me know what I'm dealing with. Any suggestions before you head back home and leave me to fend for myself?"

"Keep giving him responsibility. Let him feel needed, appreciated, it'll boost his sense of self-worth. Let him know you care. Help him feel loved and needed by you and in the community. This place is good for him. You're good for him. Take care of him Mark."

"Sure. Piece of cake," Mark said rolling his eyes. But he wasn't so sure.

CHAPTER 13

CHARLIE -
CITY CELEBRATION

The Community Building was located at the end of a road on a chunk of land next to the river. On the way, Mark filled me in about both the Community Building and the event we were about to attend.

"The local Lion's Club helped raise the money to build this Community Center. It took nearly three years," Mark said with a proud smile.

I nodded in a show of understanding.

I had never heard of such a thing as a Lion's Club, or any other group that would work together to do something for the community. I didn't know if my dad was involved in such a thing in Minneapolis or not. I felt guilty for not knowing if my own dad was involved in something like that.

"What's the Lion's Club?" I asked.

"A group I'm involved with that tries to help the community, often with building projects such as playgrounds and this Community Building. We raise money by selling calendars with everyone's birthday on it that lives in the area," Mark informed me.

He was actually beaming now. I could tell how proud he was of this Lion's Club thing. I wasn't sure why anyone would want a calendar with a bunch of birthday's on it...people you didn't know, but I didn't say anything about that.

I was glad something had gotten a smile out of Mark. He had been pretty quiet since he had gotten mad at me a couple days earlier. He knew about the trouble back home with Brian, which I had assumed. But, he also had figured out the other stuff. The conversation we had just after Dianna had left was a tough one.

"Charlie, I'm going to try really hard to understand what you're going through," Mark had told me the night before. "I know losing your mom was tough. I promise you that I will work hard to make this summer a good summer for you. But, I really..." Mark paused, searching for the right words. "I really need you to make an effort too. You know when you meet someone for the first time? Shake their hand. Look them right in the eyes and smile as you shake their hand. And...I realize that you're a little sensitive about having your hands dirty. I get it, you're a neat and tidy kid, but hey, a little dirt won't kill you will it?"

Mark was really rolling now. My feelings were split between embarrassment and relief. Relief in the fact that my secrets were out. Hiding it was a lot of work.

Mark kept on, feeling the momentum of his speech, "Let's both try to relax a bit. Have some fun this summer. You've been doing a great job with the apple trees the last few days. Neither of us is perfect and maybe we can both conquer some of our faults this summer. What do ya say?"

"Sure," I mumbled.

"Sure?" Mark said, searching for a bit more enthusiasm from me.

"Sure," I said with a little more volume.

A minute or so of awkward silence fell upon us in the truck until Mark continued. "This piece of land belonged to Mr. Weaver, a farmer who owns part of the river bottoms as well as the farm fields on the other side of the creek. The land was flood prone, usually flooded every two or three years, so it wasn't any value to him, so he sold it to the Lion's Club for one dollar.

"One dollar?" I said in amazement.

"Yeah," Said Mark, "and the Lion's Club let's people use it for wedding receptions, and other group events. Whoever uses it always donates to the Lion's Club, whatever they can afford.

"What if they don't want to donate anything, do they have to?" I asked.

"Things are different here Charlie," Mark said, pulling into the grass and gravel parking lot among other vehicles and putting his truck into park, "People try to help one another here. They make decisions not just based on what's good for them, but what's good for everyone around them."

Mark stepped out of his truck, closed the door, and strode toward a group of people standing near the entrance of the building. Again, I struggled to keep up with his long strides.

As we approached the group, everyone turned to greet Mark. Mark shook hands with one person after another in the group, and then turned to glance at me.

Turning back to the group, Mark said, "This is my nephew Charlie, Steve's kid. He's going to be staying with me for the summer. I got him helping me out a bit."

Many people stepped forward to shake my hand. I said hi to everyone and nodded and smiled to greet everyone. Mark shook hands with people as well but knowingly put his left hand on my back and made eye contact with me as I shook hands with people. I knew what he expected without him telling me. Our conversation, just minutes earlier, was enough of a reminder. I needed to smile, make eye contact, and shake hands like a normal person. Mark had been honest with me, and I saw today as my chance to show Mark that I could change.

I soon felt like everyone wanted to see the new guy in town. They probably all knew my dad and mom. It had been a while since I'd been in town and they probably knew it had something to do with my mom's death. I could feel the extra niceness they were trying to extend.

Once the little crowd that had gathered to see the new kid dispersed I followed Mark into the Community Center. It was sort of like a big open barn, but with tile flooring and cedar paneled walls inside. The big beams in the vaulted ceiling, however, reminded me of Mark's old barn. There were also bathrooms, a storage room where I assumed tables and chairs were kept, and a big kitchen that was separate to the main room, but with a large window like opening, where people were now passing crock pots, casserole dishes, and other food through to be set on tables along one wall.

There must have been one hundred people already there, mostly standing around talking. Yet many were finding places to sit.

"Let's find a table," Mark said to me and led the way between some tables.

"Hey!" Mark said as he approached a man and woman sitting at a table.

"Hey buddy!" The short man said and shook hands with Mark as he slapped him on the shoulder with his other hand.

"Charlie, this is Buster Roberts and his wife Janet," Mark said with a big smile as his friend stepped forward to greet me and his wife stood up to join him. "Buster and his family live just on the other side of the bluff from my place."

Buster couldn't have been more than 5 foot 8, not much taller than his wife. As Buster shook my hand, I could see the compact muscles in his arms push through his shirt. Buster looked to be about the same age as Mark, but his blonde hair was beginning to look more gray than blonde.

"Nice to meet you both," I said, noticing Mark's purposeful stare, waiting for me to provide his friends with the appropriate greeting.

As we sat down, Janet asked, "How is Cedar Bluff treating you so far Charlie?"

"Fine" I said, not able to think fast enough to expand upon my answer.

"Are you helping Mark keep that old house clean?" Buster asked with a loud laugh, slapping Mark on the back.

"It's not easy," I said and drew some laughs.

Feeling welcome, I listened to the conversation between Buster and Mark as I watched the people around me. Everyone seemed engaged in conversation or busy lining up food by the tables. Some older men, one wearing old overalls with an oxygen tank parked next to him started a card game at the end of one of the tables. Everyone seemed to know each other, and as more people arrived, the tables began filling up and the large room was a blur of noise. At first I was nervous about not knowing many people, but soon grew comfortable listening to Mark, Buster, and other people who stopped by our table to visit, talk about work, fishing, or the weather. I just had to field some questions about being at Mark's house, my dad, and what I've been doing to keep busy.

A man that had the appearance of being someone of importance asked for quiet, and announced that dinner would start being served in five minutes.

"Mike Nichols, our mayor," Mark whispered to me as the room grew quiet and the mayor made his announcement.

"I'll find the girls," Buster told Janet, and he joined several parents as they exited the back door of the Center.

"Shoot! Sorry Charlie, I should have told you that most of the kids were probably playing behind the building. There is some playground equipment for the younger kids and some trails through the woods and a creek as well," Mark explained.

"After dinner, you can go check it out....we won't make you do the dishes," Mark said with a grin.

Kids of all ages started coming in through the back door and joined their families at the tables. I was O.K. with Mark picking on me a bit about the dishes thing. I deserved it.

"This is Abigail, she's sixteen, and this is Emily, she's your age, thirteen," Buster said when two girls sat down, Emily across the table next to Janet and Abigail next to Buster.

I couldn't tell which girl was more beautiful. They both had the same light brown hair just like their mom. Abigail was tall, like her mom with long straight hair. She only briefly acknowledged me, but Emily said "hi" with a warm smile and continued to look in my direction as Buster told them both who I was.

"Charlie here is Mark's nephew. He's from outside Minneapolis and is going to spend the summer here in Cedar Bluff taking care of Mark," Buster said and again laughed loudly and smacked Mark on the back.

Emily continued to smile in my direction. It was hard not to look in her direction even after she looked away and began talking to her mom. She had shorter hair, but wavy like her mother. She was not nearly as tall as her older sister, and her hair was blonder, more like her dad. Buster never stopped grinning and I could tell that Emily shared his personality.

Tables of people began getting up to head to the tables to go through the line to get dinner. I followed behind Mark, Buster, and his family. It was hard not to watch Emily as we went through the line getting dinner, and Mark even elbowed me, giving me a knowing grin. I felt my face grow red, and I tried to concentrate on dinner from then on.

"Emily, why don't you take Charlie out back and introduce him to some kids your age," Janet said to Emily right after dinner.

She looked at me, then at her mom, obviously embarrassed that she should have such a task placed on her.

Oblivious of her predicament, Mark blurted out, "Yeah, and try to find Lance Bulman, Charlie should meet him," then turning to me, "Lance lives just on the other side of the bluff remember, maybe you two can hook up for some fishing this week."

"O.K." Emily replied, and getting up, motioned for me to follow her.

She headed toward the door with me trailing behind. Other kids were making their way outside, probably all receiving the same orders from their parents, "Go outside and leave us alone."

Once outside, Emily stopped and turned around, "That's Pine Creek over there. It's the creek that flows past Cedar Bluff, right across the street from Harris's Grocery, and other stores on Oak Street. Do you know where I mean?"

"Yeah, I've been there," I said.

I looked past the creek, about the same size as
Winnebago Creek that ran past Mark's house, at the woods
beyond. I could see for two hundred, if not three hundred
yards. The woods had trees, but the woods were a lot less
dense than the woods on Mark's land, the land was much
flatter, with just as much tall grass and bushes as trees.

"That's mostly bottom land," Emily said, noticing my
gaze. "It's pretty wet in there in the spring if the creek
floods, but there's hiking trails. Sometimes it's too wet to
use them though."

"Let's go see if they're catching some fish," Emily said
and walked toward a group of kids about my age who were
standing on the bank of the creek.

Joining her, we watched in awkward silence as a group
of boys were fishing. Some were using bobbers, which was
how Brian always fished. Some just had their lines in the
water, like what we did the other day with Dianna.

"What's up?" A boy said looking back, away from the
creek at Emily and me. "Who's your boyfriend?"

"Shut up," Emily said with a sneer. "This is Charlie,
Mark's nephew from Minneapolis." Then without looking
at me she said, "Charlie this is Lance, your uncle wanted
you to meet him," Then softly so only I could hear, "I
don't know why."

"Hey!" Lance said in a way that I thought was nice
enough.

"Hey." I said back.

I watched Lance reel in his line, and just a flick of his
wrist, gently deposited his bait in the water about a foot

from the far edge of the creek where the water looked the deepest.

"Want to fish?" Lance said, holding his rod out to me.

"Naw," I said.

"Sure?" Lance prodded.

"Yeah, I'll just watch," I said.

Just then two boys came over to Lance holding a couple snakes. Instinctively, I took a step back.

One of them saw my reaction and said, "Hey Lance, who's your friend?"

"Charlie, Mark's nephew from Minneapolis," Lance said, grabbing one of the snakes behind the head. "My dad said you were coming to live with Mark for the summer."

I felt nervous. I knew at any moment they would tell me to hold the snake. I turned to talk to Emily, but she was gone.

Quickly I said, "Yeah, Mark's pretty cool. I gotta go. See ya."

I headed back inside and spent the next hour listening to Mark and Buster talk about work and answering questions from Janet. I never saw Emily come back in. I wondered where she had gone. I could tell that she didn't like Lance a whole lot. He seemed cool. It was strange. Even in our brief encounter, I felt comfortable around him, sort of like I did around Brian back home.

CHAPTER 14

LANCE

It was just past noon a couple days after the celebration at the Community Building and Mark was at work. I had come back from my daily visit to the apple trees to have lunch. I'd only been with Mark for a week and only on day four of my apple tree quest, up to 14 trees trimmed, when I heard a knock on the door. It was Lance. He was dressed in jeans and a t-shirt and wearing a baseball cap and carrying two fishing rods.

"Hey, what's up?" Lance said with a big grin when I opened the screen down on the porch.

"Not much. Having some lunch. I was pruning Mark's apple trees. Just takin' a break," I said in between bites of a ham sandwich.

"Wanna go fishin?" Lance said, holding up the fishing rods, as if I didn't see them in his hands.

"I guess," I said. We grabbed a couple of sodas out of the fridge in the kitchen and I followed Lance out the door.

I was greeted by two horses, saddled and tied to Mark's front porch railing.

"Ever been on a horse before?" Lance asked with a grin.

"No," I said in reply. "What's his name?"

"Her name." Lance said. "Her name is Felicity," he said pointing at the big horse closest to me, then pointing to the smaller horse he said, "Her daughter is named Gracie."

"Are we going to ride them?" I asked, knowing instantly that it was a stupid question.

"Yep," Lance said and before I knew it he had guided me over to Gracie and was showing me how to climb on.

Lance gathered the fish poles and swung his leg over Felicity's back and commenced to telling me how to steer my horse. It wasn't too hard as I found out. Gracie just followed her mother and there wasn't a whole lot of steering involved.

We took the dirt farm road up the valley toward Mark's orchard.

"I know a good spot up stream," Lance said over his shoulder.

About 100 yards past the spot where Mark's rows of apple trees began and where I had slid of the log into the water a week earlier, we followed a deer path through the line of trees to the creek's edge, ducking under the tree branches as we went. The water looked faster here than it was under the bridge fishing with Mark and Dianna. I looked at Lance with a little uncertainty.

"Relax buddy," Lance said with a lot less arrogance than Brian would have. "See that steep bank over there? Trout like to hang tight along there. It's deeper than in the middle....and full of rocks. They like to sit behind the rocks, out of the current."

I nodded. It made sense. Besides, this was only my second time trout fishing. I had to trust Lance knew what he was doing.

Lance got off Felicity and helped me dismount Gracie and wrapped the long reins on some tree branches near a grassy spot on the edge of the creek.

I hooked a worm onto my hook thinking the whole time of Mark, imploring me to "act normal." A normal kid isn't afraid to get some worm guts on his hands. I knew that was the basis of Mark's words to me.

After only two attempts, I was able to make a good cast tight to the bank and instantly felt the tug of a fish. Excitedly I reeled it in, its silver sides catching the sunlight in the clear water. Lance grabbed it out of the shallow rocks on our side of the creek.

"Nice one!" Lance said with a big grin and tossed the trout, about a foot long, into his pail, partially filled now with water from the creek.

The rest of the morning was a lot of fun. We both caught fish. I didn't catch as many as Lance, and at times I succumbed to temptation and washed my hands in the creek, but I felt proud of myself for as Mark would say, "loosening up".

After a couple hours of fishing, Lance decided to show me his farm. Again on Gracie, Lance and Felicity led the way across the creek. It was a bit unnerving when Gracie picked her way across the fast moving water of Winnebago Creek, but the water only came to just below her knees and the young horse nimbly made it across. Then I hung on as she hopped up onto the bank.

I was having a great time, riding the beautiful brown horse up the logging road following Lance and Felicity. I even experimented with steering Gracie, but mostly just had to hang on, letting my body fall into motion with Gracie's movements as she climbed the logging road. When we crested the hill, the down slope was a bit steeper and I had to brace myself a bit by putting both hands on the saddle horn, but it was the neatest experience I had ever had.

The rest of the day consisted of watching Lance clean the trout, taking another horseback ride farther back into his parents' valley, and sitting on the fence surrounding the horse corral, drinking a Pepsi and watching the beautiful horses. Lance and I even rode a bit farther up the valley to where Emily lived. Her house was a small log home nestled amongst some trees just as the valley began to narrow and climb into the bluffs.

"That's Emily Robert's house," Lance said as he leaned forward in his saddle and pointed. "You met her at the Community Center yesterday, remember."

"Yeah sure, I guess," I said, pretending to have to recall who Emily was, when there hadn't been more than five minutes in the last 12 hours where I hadn't thought about her.

When we parted two hours later, riding the horses back over the hill, Mark greeted us in front of the house.

"Looks like you're getting a hang of this place!" said Mark with a satisfied grin.

Lance bent down from Felicity, handing me a plastic bag containing the trout and said, "Had a great time! See you Buddy!" and disappeared down the road with Gracie in tow.

Once inside, I couldn't wait to tell Mark about my awesome day.

"I caught a fish right away, made a great cast even," I said proudly.

Mostly, I wanted to talk about riding Gracie. I told him how I was learning to steer her and how we took a long ride way back into Lance's valley.

"What about the ride over the hill?" Mark asked with a proud smile I had yet to see since I had arrived.

"Not a problem. Just hung on and let Gracie do her thing," I said confidently.

"Charlie, I'll tell you what. I'm starting to see a different guy here. You didn't seem afraid one bit. It sounds like you made a good friend….and, I bet you didn't worry a lot about things today did you?"

Pausing, I said, "No, I guess I didn't."

I was being honest with Mark. All day long, I hadn't considered washing my hands, worrying about what Lance thought of me, or whether or not I needed to do anything I didn't want to. It was a great day.

CHAPTER 15

A CALL AT NIGHT

I woke to the sound of a phone ringing downstairs. I heard Mark get out of bed and go down the creaky stairs to answer the phone in the kitchen.

I could hear Mark talking but couldn't make out what he was saying. It was still dark, so I must have rolled over and fell back asleep when I woke again. This time Mark was in my room.

"Charlie. Hey bud, wake up." Mark was sitting on my bed shaking my shoulder.

"What?" I managed to say, groggily.

"Hey, I just got a call from your friend." Mark was saying in my still dark room.

"Lance?" I said as I sat up in bed.

"No. Your friend Brian." Mark answered flatly.

"Brian?" I said, confused.

"Yeah, seems your buddy made his way down to Cedar Falls somehow. He called here looking for you." Mark replied with a hint of annoyance. "He's in town...called from a gas station."

"How'd he get here?" I asked, fully awake now.

"No clue, but I said we'd go pick him up. So, get dressed." Mark said and disappeared from my room.

The ride into town consisted of questions from me and a lot of shrugs from Mark. Mark had no idea of how Brian had gotten to Cedar Falls or how he had gotten Mark's phone number. I decided to not to press him any further. I could tell he was a bit agitated. It was past midnight and the kid that my dad had blamed a lot of stuff on, whether he was right or wrong, had just called. I guess I couldn't blame Mark for being a bit grumpy.

We could see Brian standing outside wearing a backpack as Mark swung his truck into the open all night gas station just off the highway in Cedar Falls. We pulled up alongside Brian and he waved, wearing a big grin, when he saw it was me.

"Hey!" Brian called out as Mark and I got out of the truck.

Brian came right over to me, ignoring Mark and his stern look, and patted me on the shoulder with great enthusiasm.

"Hey," I replied with much less enthusiasm, sneaking a look at Mark, who now stood leaning against his truck, "How did you get here?"

"I took a bus to La Crosse, then walked on over!" Brian said as if the five mile hike across the interstate bridge spanning the Mississippi River and then along the highway in the dark was an everyday occurrence.

"Well, please tell me your parents know where you are." Mark interrupted.

"Nah, but she works early in the morning. She'll never know I'm gone. It's nothing to worry about," Brian said with a dismissing wave of his hand.

"Look, I…" Mark tried to jump in.

"If I can spend the night, we can call her in the morning. I can hang out tomorrow with Charlie, then take the bus back to Minneapolis tomorrow night," Brian said, still grinning and not a bit concerned.

"Sounds like you got it all figured out. Well, I hate to rain on your parade pal, but we're calling her now and getting you home as soon as possible," Mark said and pulled out his cell phone.

The ride back to Mark's house was a bit tense for Mark and me. Brian didn't seem the least bit worried. Mark had talked to Brian's mom, who, according to Mark, was a lot more angry than worried. Mark was also aggravated by the fact that Brian's mom said she would have to wait until after work the following day to drive the three hours down to Cedar Falls to pick Brian up.

"Look kid," Mark declared, pointing a finger at Brian as we got out of the truck in front of the old farmhouse, "You get to stay the night, just one night. I have to work tomorrow, but you can spend the day with Charlie. He's going to be working in the apple orchard. You get to help him."

"Sounds cool!" Brian said cheerily.

"Yeah, real cool!" Mark's response was loaded with sarcasm. "You can sleep on the couch in the living room."

Brian and I didn't get much chance to talk the rest of the night. Mark tossed a blanket and pillow on the living room couch and practically escorted me upstairs.

"See you in the morning," Mark said to me as he entered his own bedroom, leaving the door open.

CHAPTER 16

JUST LIKE OLD TIMES

Brian was still smiling the next morning as if hopping a bus at age thirteen without your mother knowing it and running off to visit someone a hundred miles away was no big deal. Mark didn't hide his feelings as he tossed a pancake onto Brian's plate at breakfast. Brian seemed oblivious to Mark's smoldering looks.

"Look, there is plenty for you guys to do today to keep busy," Mark said with more authority than usual, mostly for Brian's sake I think.

Once Mark left, Brian and I strolled down the dirt road toward Uncle Mark's apple trees. On the way, I explained what our task was. I actually felt pretty good informing Brian on the art of pruning apple trees. In the short amount of time I had been staying with my uncle, I had begun to take pride in my efforts. When Mark inspected my work he never once told me I was doing something wrong.

Brian thought everything about Mark's place was cool. He was only slightly interested in helping me prune the trees. I managed to entice him to take his turn on the ladder using the secateurs.

"What's over there?" Brian said, pointing to the thick
vegetation between the field and the hillside.

"It's Winnebago Creek," I said, nearly to myself, since
Brian had already starting walking in that direction.

I climbed down from the ladder and tried to catch up.

"Wait! Let's try to get some work done! We can check
out the creek later!" I said, jogging after Brian.

Ignoring me, Brian followed the trail through the tall
grass and trees, the same trail Lance and I used, just the day
before, to the creek's edge.

"Cool!" Brian said. "Are there fish in here?"

"Yeah, brown trout," I said, stepping alongside Brian.

"Ya got some poles?" Brian asked.

Nervously, I tried to reply, "Yeah, but we should…"

"Well, let's give it a shot," Brian interrupted. "It's so
shallow, where do they hang out?"

I exhaled nervously. If Brian was just interested in
fishing, I could handle that. I'd tell him about fishing
Winnebago Creek. I figured that couldn't be too bad.
Mark would probably be O.K. if we took some time to go
fishing.

Most of Brian's ideas dealt with ways to make money,
like dragging golf course ponds for golf balls. We spent
one summer sneaking out at night onto golf courses,
creeping across the course to the ponds. We would fashion
a rope to a bicycle basket and toss it in the pond and drag
in dozens of golf balls. You'd find us the next day, sitting
on a bench on the course selling balls for 25 cents, or five
for a buck.

Dragging for golf balls was kind of fun actually. Each time we pulled the basket in, it was full of golf balls. After about an hour or so, we'd have so many golf balls in our gunnysacks that we'd have to leave. The problem was, we had to sneak onto the golf course at night to "drag for golf balls." Also, Brian would get greedy. One night, we were dragging our usual ponds. We were doing pretty good, filling up the gunnysacks. Then Brian decided that we needed to drag a pond too close to the club house. We ended up getting chased that night by guys on golf carts. We had run up into the hill to escape, lost most of our golf balls, and ended up climbing a tree to hide. It seemed like every time Brian has a great idea, I end up getting chased through the woods, and end up sitting in a tree in the dark. But, I couldn't imagine that doing a little fishing could get us into too much trouble.

"Well, I suppose we can try to catch a couple. See that deeper spot near the bank?" I said pointing. "That's where we'll get them. Let's head back to the house and get the fishing poles."

"Wait!" Brian said, putting his hand up to stop me. "Are you saying the fish are right in that little hole?"

Before I could answer, Brian said, "Let's just build a wall with rocks below their hole and trap them there. Then we just have to reach in and grab em'. Or...I can do it. I know how you hate to get your hands dirty," Brian continued with a smirk.

Brian jumped right into stacking rocks in the shallow water just below the deeper hole Lance and I had fished, stopping the flow of the creek. I joined in, but not at quite the same pace as Brian.

"There!" Brian exclaimed, standing back to admire his dam building skills. "Let's come back in a little bit, once the water has run out below, and we'll grab our fish."

"Fine, let's finish our pruning," I said, determined to redirect Brian. But, he had other ideas.

"Nah! Let's follow this trail," Brian said and off he went again, jumping up onto the opposite bank and following the old logging road up the hill.

Again, I felt forced to follow him. Besides, I knew the trail, the same one Mark and my dad walked, and the same one Lance I took with the horses.

"Where does this go?" Brian asked pausing just long enough in his uphill hike to inquire.

"Up over the hill to my friend Lance's farm," I told him. "We rode horses on this trail yesterday."

"You rode a horse? Yeah, right! Did you have to give it a bath first?!" Brian joked.

"Very funny," I said with a frown.

"Let's check out the horses!" Brian shouted.

So we went up over the hill on the logging road. I was fine with showing Brian Lance's horses. Lance wouldn't mind. Maybe he would be home and I could show Brian how I can ride Gracie. If Brian was going to poke fun at me for my quirks, I'd show him what I could do, maybe shut him up a bit.

As we came down the hill and within view of the Bulman family's corral of horses, Brian took off at a run.

Before I knew it, he was perched on the top rail of the corral.

"Can we ride them?" Brian asked.

"Maybe. I'll go see if Lance is home and find out," I said.

I was almost to Lance's front door, when I looked back at the corral. I stopped short and gasped at what I saw. Brian had already made his decision. He was going to try to ride a horse. He managed to open the gate to the corral and was inside trying to catch Felicity. Behind him, six other horses were exiting from the open gate.

"Hey!" I heard a shout and turned to see George Bulman, Lance, and Lance's two brothers standing on the porch looking past me to the corral.

"Who's that kid and what's he doing with the horses?!" shouted Mr. Bulman.

Before I could answer, the Bulman family had jogged over to the corral and were beginning to round up their horses.

We spent the next hour or so catching some of the skittish young mares. Brian thought it was a fun time. Lance, his brothers, and his father weren't too happy.

"If you want to ride my horses, just ask," was all Lance said to me.

"You and your buddy better go home now," George Bulman said with an angry frown once the mares were put back safely.

CHAPTER 17

MARK AND THE BATTLE JUST STARTING

Sitting on the porch that night watching the thunderstorm roll in, Mark talked to his brother on the phone. Dinner with Charlie was without much conversation. Instead of talking about Charlie's exciting progress with the apple trees and the wildlife that Charlie saw during the day as he worked, they both sat in relative silence, Charlie fighting back tears the whole time. The phone call to Steve was going to be a tough one.

"Steve, hey it's Mark."

"Hey! Good news!" Steve didn't let Mark share the bad news about Charlie quite yet.

"Hang on Steve, I…," Mark tried to say.

Steve continued on, "It's a done deal. I accepted the job in La Crosse, right across the river. I'm still working for the same parent company, still able to stay in investments, and I'm going to do it. I'll have to start from scratch as far as my clientele, but I think I can use some of my business contacts to make the transition easier. Think you can handle having me as a roommate, like you said."

"Yeah! Sounds great!" Mark said, trying to sound enthusiastic for his brother's sake.

They had talked about this for the past week and a half, and although Mark didn't think it would happen so quickly, Steve had decided that it was time to move back home. For Charlie's sake. It had been going so good for the short time that Charlie had been here, up until now, and both brothers had become more and more excited about it.

"And!" Steve continued, "I have an offer in to buy part of that upper valley from Ronnie Dunn. That would give you another 60 acres up the valley, more than enough to put in some apple trees, and make a real business out of it. I figure the equity I have in my house should make a nice down payment, and I have plenty in savings, to get us started with all the necessary machinery. I think Ronnie will go for the offer. He's not even using it for crops right now. What do you think....partner?"

Mark hesitated. Not because of Steve's news. That was great. That was what they both had hoped for. Their plan was coming together, and quickly. Mark's hesitation was because he hated to throw a wrench into things by having to tell Steve about Charlie.

"Steve, that's great. It really is. And believe me, I'm just as excited as you are. I sure do appreciate you jumping in with me on the orchard thing. I couldn't do it without you. I can carry the work load, while you continue on with your career.

Thanks for trusting me enough to back me financially on this. That extra acreage will make the difference. But, we had a little difficulty today....with Charlie that is," Mark said feeling awful that he had to disrupt the good news with a big chunk of bad.

"Oh no," Steve said on the other end of the phone. He let out a big sigh, "What is it?"

"Well," Mark said, "Charlie's little buddy Brian called late last night. Seems he took a bus to La Crosse last night, then walked over to Cedar Bluff. He called shortly after midnight and I went to pick him up in town."

"Ahh!" Steve responded on the other end of the line. "Did he run away from home or what?"

"Well, his mom knew nothing about it, if that's what you mean. Then while I was at work today, the kid convinced Charlie to amble over to the Bulman's where they were messing around with some of their horses. Not a big problem, George and his boys had to round up a few of their mares that Brian and Charlie let out," Mark delivered the story to his brother.

Another big sigh from the other end of the line, and Mark could almost feel the disappointment through the phone.

"Well, then when I came home, I found part of my orchard flooded," continued Mark. "Seems they thought it was a good idea to use some rocks to dam up the creek. The creek jumped its bank and ran out into the orchard."

"I'm sorry Mark. I was hoping we were turning a corner with Charlie. Do I need to come down there and sort it out with George Bulman? Or....do I need to come down and pick both boys up and take them back home with me?" said Charlie's father, sounding exasperated.

"No," Mark continued. "George was a bit upset, but I calmed him down some."

"George is a good man," Charlie's father continued. "Do I owe anything for damages?"

"Horses were put back in good shape and no major flood damage to the apple trees. We caught it in time or half the orchard would have been under water, so I think we're O.K." Mark said.

Did Charlie apologize?" Steve asked.

"Yeah, and he's been crying since I got home. Brian's mom picked him up a little while ago and took him back home, so that will certainly help. He was doing so good until today," Mark said, trying to lighten his brother's obvious disappointment. "He's been a great help pruning the apple trees. I even took him fishing with Dianna. Look, Steve, I think he made a mistake. I have to belief it's isolated. That kid Brian surely didn't help things."

Steve burst in, "I've said that several times. It's an isolated thing. He won't do it again. But…he always does something dumb later on, especially when Brian is part of the picture."

"Well, sounds like with your great news, we won't have to worry about that anymore, will we?" Mark said, trying to sound upbeat.

"Well, who's to say Charlie won't meet some other kid and they team up to cause trouble in Cedar Falls?" Steve inquired.

Mark tried to sound optimistic, "Look, Charlie's come a long way in a short time. He hung out with Lance Bulman just yesterday. They went fishing, horseback

riding, had a great time. Charlie even admitted that he
spent the whole day not worrying about anything. Not
about getting dirty, trying to fit in, all that compulsive stuff.
He just hung out with another kid and they had a great
time."

"Yeah, well maybe it's coming together for him.
Sounds like you've noticed all the different things with
Charlie," Steve said.

"I have," Mark replied, "But, you know, I figure the
kid can get past all that stuff."

"Thanks. I hope so." Steve said, "Can I talk to
Charlie?"

When Charlie took the phone, Mark sat next to him
and watched the emotions flow as he talked to his father.
Charlie cried steadily during the entire conversation. He
pleaded with his father to give him another chance. After a
minute or so, Charlie handed the phone back to Mark and
headed up to his room.

"Well, what do you think?" Steve asked his brother.

"I think he's a good kid," Mark declared. "You know
Dianna is a pediatrician right? Well, she thinks he has some
Obsessive Compulsive thing going on."

"Yeah, I figured something like that was going on,"
Steve said, "But, I guess I hoped he'd outgrow it, or we'd
figure out how to deal with it."

Mark continued, "Dianna is going to help us out Steve.
She's going to help us get connected with someone who
can help. We'll help the kid out."

"Thanks Mark. Thanks for everything," Steve said.

"Look, I'm heading there first thing in the morning. I need

to square away a couple things with the new job anyway. I'll see you tomorrow around noon. You might want to keep the move quiet for now, until it's a done deal."

"Sound good. Tomorrow. Gotcha. And hey!" Mark said, "This will work. I'm confident."

Mark left the porch and went back inside. He'd take Charlie over to La Crosse to a movie. The thought of sitting around with Charlie alone with all the stress in the house from the day's events didn't appeal to him. At least in the movies, they could sit in silence and not feel the pressure to talk.

Charlie agreed to go with just a solemn, "sure".

As they climbed into the old Chevy, the wind was picking up and the rain came down more steadily and Mark turned his wipers on high.

Mark wasn't lying to his brother. Things weren't all bad. Things would work out, hopefully.

Driving, the silence was too much for Mark.

"Hey pal," Mark finally said as he guided his truck past Cedar Bluff, and turned to go over the bridge over the Mississippi to enter La Crosse, Wisconsin. "Look let's move on past this whole thing, O.K.? I know things are tough for you. I cared about your mom too. This whole thing with the hand washing and all that, well, I think you can get past that too. But you know... making bad decisions can give you dirty hands too. Let's start fresh tomorrow."

Mark gave a faint smile and gave Charlie a gentle shove. A feeble smile and a nod was the only response he could get from his troubled nephew.

CHAPTER 18

THE RAIN

When we came out of the movie theater, we saw that the rain hadn't slowed at all. It was now coming down in sheets, soaking us as we sprinted to the truck.

"Wow!" Mark exclaimed as he shook the water from his dark, curly hair when we were sitting in his truck, winded from the sprint through the rain, dodging puddles and the flowing water along the curb.

"It's really raining." I said in reply.

The movie, a comedy, had calmed me down a bit. We had munched popcorn and sipped sodas as we laughed. It had loosened us both up a bit. We even talked about the movie and laughed some as Mark drove his truck back over the bridge into Minnesota. The mood changed when the weather report came over the radio.

Flash flood warnings were being posted for all small rivers and streams. Five inches of rain had fallen over the last couple hours and evacuations were already in process in low lying areas.

"Shh! Shh!" Mark said and turned up the radio, interrupting our conversation.

Immediately Mark's mood turned serious as he pulled out his cell phone and began dialing.

"Buster, it's Mark….yeah, no I've been at the movies…jeez that's a lot of rain." Mark said in his rushed conversation with his friend Buster.

"O.K." Mark said, pausing as he listened to Buster on the other line. "Well, I'll be there in ten minutes."

Mark shut off his phone and tossed it on the dash of his truck, frowning.

"We certainly got a great big bunch of rain while we sat in the theater," Mark said. "We still should be able to get to our house. As of right now, our road is still open. We'll hustle and check things out."

I could sense my uncle's concern. Remembering the conversation he had with my dad while checking out his land when I first arrived made me worry. Mark was worried. He had also talked about how the barn had once been taken by the creek. Mark's urgency was apparent as he picked up the pace in his truck, water splashing up on both sides of his truck as he drove down the rain soaked highway hitting big puddles in low spots in the road.

"Will the creek flood?" I finally asked Mark as we began driving down the county road that heads toward Winnebago Valley. Mark's silence was beginning to make me nervous.

"Could," Mark responded as he wiped the steam off the inside of his windshield with his hand. "Usually we have flooding problems in April or May after the snow melts off up north, at least that's when the Mississippi rises. But, these little creeks fill up fast in a big rain, so we'll head home. If we have to evacuate the valley, at least we can grab some things…clothes, pictures, you know, just in case."

I tried to see outside the truck, tried to look at what everything looked like as we drove but the darkness, trees, and blinding rain stopped me from seeing anything. Five inches of rain sounded like a lot, and the feel of the truck sliding a bit each time we hit a big patch of water on the road was unnerving.

Then, straight ahead we saw the lights. Through the rain, we saw many lights clumped together, not moving on the highway.

"Oh, Oh," Mark mumbled as he slowed down. A line of five or six cars had stopped along the highway. A couple cars were turning around. A squad car was parked in the middle of the road, it lights flashing. Some people in the cars ahead of us were getting out. I could see the police officer talking to people and began to head our way.

"Mark," said the police officer to Mark, rain pouring off his baseball hat, as Mark rolled down his window. "All the creeks are rising in a hurry and part of the hillside came down over the highway just ahead."

"Can we get through Todd?" Mark asked.

The police officer thought for a moment.

"Look Mark," The officer said hastily, "I'm making everyone turn around, too much mud and debris on the highway. A lot of small creeks are out of their banks and Doug just said on the radio that there are multiple roads out ahead.

"I just have a little ways until my road, Todd. We've been in La Crosse tonight. I had no idea how much rain we were getting. I just need to get home, grab a few things, in case I need to evacuate the valley," Mark said firmly.

"How's your four wheel drive?" The officer said with a sigh, shaking his head.

"Good." Mark said flatly.

"Go for it then," The officer said, "But be careful and keep moving, or you'll never make it."

"Thanks Todd," Mark said and pulled his truck to the shoulder on the right and passed the five or six cars ahead of him, that were now beginning to turn around.

What a mess. In Mark's headlights, I could see what had happened. The steep hillside to the right of the highway had given way. In our lane, a big wall of mud lay in the road, probably five feet tall and stretching down the highway farther than I could see in the rain. In the opposite lane, the mud didn't appear to be as deep, but was littered with a tangle of small trees and rocks. It looked impenetrable. We started out slow, working our way through the mud on the road. Right away, Mark had to swing way to the left shoulder of the road to stay where it was not so thick and to avoid a bush or some sort of small tree sticking out of the mud. Suddenly, I could feel the truck's wheels spin and the whole back end of the truck started swinging back and forth.

"Hold tight!" Mark said sharply and accelerated, trying to keep our momentum going forward.

Through the driving rain, I could see something big, a whole end of a tree directly ahead of us. We were really spinning now, the engine screaming as Mark fought the wheel to keep us going straight. Mud flew up on the side windows and I could hear and feel the debris sliding and spraying the bottom of his truck. The tree was only 30 feet ahead of us now, and Mark was trying to turn the truck to avoid it. But, every time Mark tried to nudge the truck to the right, the whole rear end slid around and Mark had to correct it by straightening it out. We had no choice but to go right through the branches.

"Oomph," I heard myself say as I bounced around in the cab, grabbing onto the dash board to hold myself upright and the truck busted through the branches, still spinning and sliding in the thick mud. We almost came to a complete stop, probably hitting the trunk or a bigger branch underneath the mud.

"Get going," Mark said between gritted teeth and slammed the accelerator to the boards.

With a roar of the engine and a thump that bounced my head off the top of the cab, we rammed over and through the branches of the tree. Still sliding and spinning, we came through the last of the mud and made it through the mudslide, onto clear pavement, where Mark finally stopped his truck.

Mark got out to inspect his truck. I was too curious to stay inside, even with the pouring rain, and joined him in the front of his truck to look for damage. The truck was completely covered in mud. Steam came up from underneath the truck from the mud and rain on the hot engine block. The pouring rain was already rinsing it off, big wet globs of mud sliding off the sides and plopping onto the ground.

"That was pretty dicey, but I think we're O.K. I'd look underneath, but she's pretty caked full of mud, doubt I'd be able to see anything anyway. Let's go," Mark said and jumped back in his truck.

Just a mile or so past the mess in the road, we turned onto Mark's road and sped up the valley. The truck bounced around a lot as we hit potholes filled with water, sending water splashing up onto the windshield.

When Mark skidded to a stop next to his house, Mark scrambled from the truck cab without speaking and hurried inside. I followed. Mark was again on his cell phone, taking just a second to direct an order my way.

"Run up stairs and throw some clothes in a bag," Mark said quickly, and then turned his attention to his phone.

"Buster, yeah, it's me. O.K. Charlie's packing a bag. Yeah, I know, but I really need to see how close the creek is to swallowing up my trees. I know, I know," Mark argued briefly and then hung up.

"Charlie!" Mark yelled, thinking I was upstairs packing. My nervousness had made we wait part way up the stairs so I could hear Mark's phone conversation. I was anxious to find out how much trouble we were in.

"Charlie! Keep packing!" Mark yelled up the stairs again. "I'll be right back. I need to run up the valley and check on something."

I stood in the narrow stairwell. One part of me wanted to grab my things, throw it all in my suitcase and get ready to head for high ground. The other part of me took over and I ran down the steps, out the door and into the rain.

I ran trying to catch Mark. He was already out of sight, hidden in the darkness and pouring rain. He told Buster he was going to check on his apple trees, so I ran, almost blindly, down the dirt road along the corn field heading up the valley. As I ran I thought that I would catch Mark and have to explain myself, but I reached the end of the corn field and the start of the apple orchard without having seen Mark. I stopped and listened, standing in the dark, in the rain, straining to hear or see where he was.

In the moment that I stood there looking, I felt a funny feeling on my legs. Looking down, I realized that the creek had already jumped its banks and what I felt on my legs was the water, ankle deep, swirling around me.

I looked up for Mark again. A flash of lightning came at the right time. There he was. In the short burst of light I saw him only forty yards away, between the apple trees and the little band of trees that ran along the creek. I headed toward him, slipping as I went in the mud that had become the road, practically using the silhouette of the apple trees to lead me along its edge.

When I finally could see him, he was hunched over, shovel in hand. Where Mark stood, he was uphill a bit from the start of the apple trees and I saw that the water had not yet climbed to that elevation.

He was frantically digging up dirt from the high ground and throwing into a heap along a row, trying to create a small, dirt barricade to keep the water out of his orchard.

"Uncle Mark, the water keeps washing away the dirt faster than you can pile it." I said, realizing at once that I had made a very apparent observation.

"Here! Keep shoveling," shouted Mark through the rain, as he pulled out his cell phone.

This time I didn't try to listen in. I started shoveling as I had seen Mark do, filling the shovel with the muddy soil and heaving it into a row as fast as I could.

"Help is on the way." Mark said with a gasp and pulled the shovel from my hand. "Run back and grab another shovel and the wheelbarrow from the barn!"

"Shouldn't we...?" But the look on Mark's face, even in the dark, gave me the answer.

I turned and ran back toward the house. Mark had no plans to run from the creek. He was going to stay and fight for his trees.

I threw open the barn door and wiping the water from my eyes, felt along the wall for the light switch. Finding the wheelbarrow, I tossed a spade into the metal bottom and steered the wheelbarrow out into the rain and up the road, slipping and sliding in the mud as I struggled to keep it moving in the right direction.

CHAPTER 19

THINKING OF OTHERS

Back alongside Mark, I started digging, filling the wheelbarrow with Mark, then pausing while he dumped the dirt into a series of piles next to the row of trees along the road, now under water. With each lightning flash I could see the water engulfing the narrow band of trees between the submerged road and the trees. We soon could no longer stand in the road to shovel the dirt; the water had grown to a foot deep. We were forced to retreat in amongst the first row of little apple trees.

"Charlie, you had better take off. Head back... grab your bag... walk up the hill behind my house. You'll be safe there." Mark said between gasps.

"No," I said back. "I'll be..."

But my voice trailed off. Looking across the creek in the driving rain, I could see lights heading down the hill, angling toward the little bridge, just upstream.

"Mark, there's lights," I said, pointing across the creek to the hillside.

"That should be George Bulman and Buster," Mark yelled back through the darkness and rain. They're hopefully bringing a couple wagon loads of sand and gravel, along with Buster's front end loader, but I only see one set of lights."

As I shoveled, I watched the lights run upstream, parallel with the creek, still heading downhill. The lights then turned and angled more toward us, flickering a little bit, and then I knew they were crossing the bridge and heading back toward us.

Neither of us stopped shoveling, barely able to fill a spot in our row of dirt, before the water breached another spot. The hole we had created by stealing dirt to build the make shift water, was now filled with water, and we sloshed in the mud as we moved back and forth.

Soon we could hear even through the rain, the roar of a tractor, and then they were here. It was George Bulman, Lance, and his two brothers, David and Tom. With Lance and his brothers riding on top of a wagon load of sand and gravel, their father drove the tractor over a couple small apple trees, into the muddy water, and pulled alongside our failing dike. Immediately, Lance and his brothers started shoveling off the fill, trying to reinforce the work Mark and I had done.

Then I felt some arms around me and Mark was lifting me into the wagon with the others.

"Start shoveling off the fill, as George pulls forward!" Mark yelled. "George, is Buster coming?!"

"On his way!" shouted Mr. Bulman over the roar of the tractor.

Mark joined us on top of the wagon and with five shovels working, we tried to catch up with the rising creek.

The urgency of it all gave me no time to worry about mud, dirt, and the fact that I was soaking wet. Everyone was working frantically. My arms and back were soon aching and my hands felt raw from the sand and the shovel handle.

Soon, I could see that the fifty feet of low area that we needed to seal off was sectioned off by our little wall.

Minutes later, we could again see another set of lights winding down the logging road on the hillside across from us.

"I think we did it," Lance said, noticing that our wall was holding and the rain had let up.

"Not yet, the valley is still emptying. We're not out the woods yet," came the cautious response.

"Here comes Buster with his front end loader!" Mark shouted.

We kept shoveling as we watched the lights begin to cross the bridge upstream. The lights stopped part way across. As we watched, Mark stopped throwing fill off the wagon, stood straight up, and swore just loud enough to be heard.

Then I could see what caused his reaction. The lights began to angle a bit, and then the lights began backing up. Just then, all in the same moment, the lights tipped toward the water, falling down, as a figure could be seen passing in front of the lights. Even in the dark, even in the rain, we all knew that the bridge had failed under the weight of the loader and its riders were jumping clear.

Mr. Bulman and Mark leaped off the wagon and splashed into the water, wading out waist deep, using trees to keep from being swept downstream, trying to get to the creek's main flow.

Instinctively, Lance, his brothers, and I jumped in behind them. We waded out as well, following the men, knowing that whoever jumped free of the tractor may be flowing past any second.

Suddenly, I saw, something coming quickly toward us out in the main part of the creek. It was a person, splashing hard, battling the pull of the water. One of the men ahead of me shouted and lunged in that direction, trying to grab the person. Mr. Bulman, Mark, and the others all missed; the person was being carried too fast in the swirling water.

My father always accused me of acting without thinking. I just did it. I plunged forward in the water toward the person. The power of the water was incredible. I struggled to get my bearings, feeling my body tear past trees and brush. I took a moment to right my body into a swimming position, and pulled hard with my arms, trying to steer myself in the direction I last saw the person.

Then I saw what I was looking for, the frantic splashing of arms fighting to keep the body above water. In the darkness, I could see the person's head only, sticking out of the swirling water of the creek, coming at me fast.

The water was congested with debris as I worked to keep myself moving in the right direction in the strong current.

Even with the roar of the water I could hear the shouts of people behind me, yelling my name.

The person heard the shouts too, and turned my way. It was Emily. I never considered the fact that she would be with her father, coming across the bluff to help.

Without taking my eyes off her, I could see the speed at which we were travelling, quickly past the wooded shoreline. I could no longer tell where the creek bed was, the creek seemed huge, a muddy flow, tearing through trees. Judging by the lack of trees I was flowing through, I had to be in the main creek bed.

As I came closer to Emily, swimming with my head up to keep her in sight, she continued to struggle, but beginning to have moments when her head disappeared under the muddy water.

With a furious burst of speed I caught her, crashed into her actually, my chest slamming into her back, my face hitting her wet, matted hair. Startled, she turned slightly. I will always remember the look in her eyes. Even in the darkness, I saw her fear, exhaustion, confusion. She tried to say something, mouthing something I couldn't understand.

Breathing hard, I hooked one arm around her chest, underneath her right arm and pulled hard with my left arm trying to angle toward what I hoped was water free of the creek flow. Kicking hard, my legs were battered underneath the water by branches and other objects lurking under the dark, frothy water.

With the added weight, I fought to keep my own head above water, submerging myself with each pull of my arm through the water, using my hip to keep Emily's head above the surface. By chance I looked downstream in time to see a tree standing upright in our path. I only had a split second to adjust my body for the collision, taking the force of the impact with my shoulder. Pain instantly shot through my entire arm. Yet, I was able to grab on, the force of the water spinning the both of us to the leeward side of the tree.

"Grab the tree!" I shouted to Emily.

Weakly she stretched her arms out and fought for a handhold. Then I felt it. Ground underneath my feet. We were out of the creek bed. The tree was on shore. I tried hard to get a foot hold in the chest deep rushing water, both arms around Emily, my hands grasping for a grip on the tree. Looking up I could see a branch, coming straight out from the tree, just out of my reach. I had to grab that branch. Emily was having trouble hanging on; the weight being pushed against me was becoming too much.

As my feet struggled to keep us upright, my knee made contact with something under water. Whatever it was, a branch, a rock, I forced my leg through the flow of the water and stepped on it. It was solid. Again hooking one arm around Emily, I let go of the tree with the other arm and lunged for the branch, pushing off the underwater object with my leg. I grabbed on and pulled, pinning Emily to the tree with my legs. I felt her bear hug the tree trunk with all her might, my right arm still hanging on to her sweatshirt. My legs were searching now, finding a firmer hold.

"Hang on to me!" I shouted, my voice strained by the weight of my passenger and the pull of the water. We both hung on tight, my legs constantly trying to gain hold on the branches of the tree, my arms around Emily, pinning her to the tree.

"Are you O.K.?" I managed to whisper, her head pinned against my shoulder.

"Yeah," Came her winded response.

What may have been five minutes felt like ten times that, I heard shouts and the roar of a tractor motor. I tried to shout back, but my voice was weak. Emily made no attempt, her strength beginning to fade.

Soon lights shined in our direction. I managed to quickly wave an arm, not daring to release my grip of the tree. Whoever was on the tractor saw us and I watched as the tractor, now without it's wagon, push through the water and flooded vegetation toward us until the water grew too deep and too fast. In the darkness, I could see Mark, climb off into the water and pick his way toward us in the neck deep water, using trees to keep him upright.

"Everybody O.K.?" I heard the shout as Mark drew near.

Still winded I was able to say, "Yeah" which came out raspy and high pitched.

Mark's strong arms first grabbed Emily and he dragged her through the water toward the tractor. A moment later he came back for me and together we picked our way through the flooded timber to the tractor.

Emily was already up on the tractor, being held on by George Bulman. Mark and I walked out behind the tractor, stumbling over debris as the water grew shallower.

Once we made it back to the soggy, muddy road, I saw that the road was half swallowed by the high water, and in the darkness and mud, people were waiting for us.

Buster was there with Janet, Abigail, Lance, and his brothers. Emily was immediately swept up in his arms, her face buried in his strong chest.

George Bulman came down from his tractor, his face close to mine, "You alright son?"

"Yeah, I'm fine." I said.

"You both gave us a scare," Mark said. "We weren't sure if you were able to catch up with Emily. Buster, Janet, and Abigail were able to scramble to the bank quick enough, but Emily got caught up in the flow. Good job Charlie."

I nodded and felt the slap on my back as Buster finally released his daughter long enough to give me a big thank you shake, and Janet gave me a big hug.

I couldn't help but laugh a little to myself. Those couple times where Brian had us climb a tree to escape from being caught doing something stupid, I never once thought climbing one would save my life.

"What's so funny?" It was Emily, seeing my smile and speaking for the first time.

"Nothing," I said, still smiling.

"Thanks," Emily said, just loud enough for me to hear.

CHAPTER 20

CHARLIE'S REDEMPTION

The men went back to their dike for a bit after the swim Emily and I took. The work we had done with the fill was enough to keep most of the water out of the apple orchard. Buster's loader was seen sitting in the water up against some trees. The rest of us went back to Mark's house to dry off and make some coffee.

However, just as quickly as the creek rose, it dropped back down, finally settling back into its banks. When Mark, Buster, and George returned just after sunrise, we were still awake, listening to the radio and hearing that we were not the only ones to have experienced an action packed evening.

News reports said that overnight an unbelievable ten inches of rain fell. They said the ground was so saturated, that anymore rains in the next couple days would send the creek out of its banks again.

Emily sat by me on the couch until first light, watching T.V. and waiting for her father to return. Her smile and having her close made me glad I was impulsive enough to jump in after her.

Nobody mentioned my problems with Brian from the day before, and George Bulman didn't give any indication of bringing it up. I certainly appreciated that!

As we all had some breakfast, Lance's family, Emily's family, Mark and I, sitting together around the kitchen, the aches and pains from the mornings activities set in. My shoulders hurt. My back hurt. Even my hands hurt. But it was a good ache. It was a good pain. I felt good about my efforts. I knew that this was a big day for me. I grimaced and smiled at the same time as I got up to help with the dishes. I had beaten back some fears, some temptations, and it was a battle inside me that I wasn't sure I'd ever win.

We had saved most of the orchard and the neighboring corn field. Thinking about the hug I got from Emily's mom, the big smack on the back from Buster, and the friendly way George Bulman put his arm around me after my swim was as just as reassuring as my personal triumph.

Suddenly, the door opened.

"Dad!" I yelled. "What are you doing here?"

"Mark called a few hours ago and told me about your adventure. So, I hopped in my car at four in the morning, and came on down. Mark told me about your little swim. It sounds like you're the big hero!" My father said proudly.

"Although, I hear yesterday wasn't so good," he said, his demeanor turning more serious.

"You know what, let's not worry about yesterday," Mark said as he came forward to shake his brothers hand. Charlie here has washed his hands of all his problems...it was quite a bath actually. Things are going to change for all of us. Steve, I think you have some good news to share with Charlie."

My stay with Uncle Mark was going to be permanent.

My dad was going to join us as soon as he could and I knew, especially when I saw the smiles from my new neighbors that for once everything was going to work out.

ABOUT THE AUTHOR

Jon Steffes is an elementary teacher in La Crescent, Minnesota. Growing up and living alongside the Mississippi River, he has always felt fortunate to have hunting and fishing opportunities just down the road. The beautiful valleys around La Crescent, each with its own small river or creek, inspired Jon to base his first novel in a similar setting.

Jon's next novel will be about the Armistice Day storm of 1940, which his father survived, and took the lives of many duck hunters in and near Winona, Minnesota.